About *Anonymous*

"Every so often, God develops a life to whom God can pull back the veil and entrust a revelation that is revolutionary in its nature. God has developed such a person in Alicia Chole and through her has communicated a truth that speaks to every segment in the Body of Christ. Whether you are a pastor or lay member, seasoned saint or initial convert, you will find yourself being lovingly corrected and encouraged in terms of the obscure and frustrating parts of your life's journey. You'll be encouraged to know that it isn't a matter of the terrain; it's a matter of the company. You'll come to understand and embrace the anonymous and hidden times as God's time of developing an unshakeable identity, disciplined imagination, and submission-based authority. It is a must read for anyone who takes the path to maturity in Christ seriously."

Dr. Claude R. Alexander Jr.,
Pastor, University Park Baptist Church, www.upbc.org

"Why do I recommend this book? In the first place, because it is true. Second, because it is Biblical. Third, because Alicia is a gifted wordsmith. Lastly, I like the book because it is vulnerable. I can not recommend this book more highly. You will not regret having read it. Don't read it rapidly. Read it slowly. Mull it over and let the book mull you over."

Dr. Bill Taylor, World Evangelical Alliance, Global Ambassador

Alicia Chole has a unique way of framing truth. Her heartfelt and thoughtful words in *Anonymous* penetrate the soul and make you feel and think in new ways. And when I read what Alicia has written, I don't just feel like I know her. I feel like she knows me.

Mark Batterson, author of *In a Pit with a Lion on a Snowy Day*.
Lead Pastor of National Community Church, Washington, DC
www.markbatterson.com

Anonymous makes sense out of those times in life when we feel that God is violating our rights—our right to be well-known, our right to be important, our right to be fulfilled. In our culture, celebrity and busyness have become diseases that are killing us. Alicia's excellent book is the best therapy I know of. It is full of wisdom without formulas and grace without compromise.

Earl Creps, author of *Off-Road Disciplines*, www.earlcreps.com

Alicia is one of those rare communicators who captures the hearts and challenges the minds of a generation. With words of a poet, skillful precision, and uncommon insight her writing gives utterance to what our hearts intuitively know and long to tell. Her book, *Anonymous*, sits on my shelf next to C.S. Lewis and I am convinced that someday she will rise to a similar prominence if given the platform and freedom to express her full God given potential.

Jennifer Rothschild, author of *Lessons I Learned in The Dark*,
Self Talk, Soul Talk, www.jenniferrothschild.com

In a culture obsessed with 15 minutes of Fame, Alicia brings ancient truth to life in her work *Anonymous*. Her insights on Jesus' "hidden years" serve as a map through the essential times of spiritual deserts where true character is forged and revealed. This book reminds us that—in the wastelands—nothing is ever wasted. This is a modern classic from the pen of the seeker's companion.

Anita Renfroe, author, comedian, fellow pilgrim, www.anitarenfroe.com

I was profoundly moved by *Anonymous*. This is one of those books that we as Christ-followers deeply need to read but aren't necessarily given the opportunity to read. The emphasis on character more than accomplishment and the profound joy that can be found in being, well, anonymous, are messages that affected me deeply. I am so thankful that this book was written.

Jay Kelly, President and Co-Founder, www.leadershipbuzz.com

How can I say it? Stunning. Brilliant. Penetrating. Incredibly insightful. A perspective of the temptation and hidden years of Jesus I don't think anyone has seen as clearly as you have. It should become a Christian classic. I pray for its wide readership. You have given a great gift to the Body of Christ.

Dr. George Wood, General Superindentent, Assemblies of God

Leave behind the stained-glass images of Jesus, the stereotypical cliches, the chrurch pageants and enter the pages of Alicia Britt Chole's *Anonymous*! This provocative, creative work allows one to glimpse the Jesus we long to view. A Savior, fully man, yet fully God. Christ growing up, cutting teeth, studying the Jewish faith, learning His father's trade, walking through the dusty streets unnoticed for most of his life. In Chole's writing I rejoice with new insight at how God's Son became the Son of Man, and am inspired with renewed passion to follow in His beautifully authentic footsteps.

Bonnie Keen, Author/Speaker/Recording Artist, www.bonniekeen.com

anonymous

Jesus'

hidden years . . .

and yours

alicia britt chole

THOMAS NELSON
Since 1798

NASHVILLE   DALLAS   MEXICO CITY   RIO DE JANEIRO

To Barry,

my beloved husband, dearest friend, and wisest mentor:

a man who in faith treasures the unseen potential of every hidden soul.

In the spirit of Barnabas, you invest in others richly

then with joy step back to watch them shine.

Published in Nashville, Tennessee, by Thomas Nelson. Thomas Nelson is a registered trademark of Thomas Nelson, Inc.

Thomas Nelson, Inc. books may be purchased in bulk for educational, business, fund-raising, or sales promotional use. For information, please e-mail SpecialMarkets@ThomasNelson.com.

Published in association with the literary agency of Alive Communications, Inc., 7680 Goddard Street, Suite 200, Colorado Springs, Colorado, 80920.

Except where otherwise indicated, Scripture quotations are taken from The Holy Bible, New International Version® (NIV®). Copyright © 1973, 1978, 1984 by International Bible Society. Used by permission of Zondervan. All rights reserved. Scripture quotations indicated KJV are from the Authorized King James Version of the Bible.

Cover Design: Brand Navigation, LLC—DeAnna Pierce, Bill Chiaravalle,
    www.brandnavigation.com.
Cover Photo: Photonica—Joshua Sheldon
Author Photo: Randy Bacon, www.randybacon.com
Interior Design: Susan Browne Design

For more information about the author and her ministry, visit *www.truthportraits.com.*

ISBN: 978-0-7852-9839-7 (tp)

Library of Congress Cataloging-in-Publication Data

Chole, Alicia Britt.
  Anonymous / by Alicia Britt Chole.
      p. cm.
  Summary: "Using Christ's first twenty-nine years of life as a comparison, Alicia Chole shows us that being anonymous doesn't mean being unimportant"—Provided by publisher.
  ISBN: 978-1-59145-421-2 (hc)
  1. Jesus Christ—Biography—Meditations. 2. Jesus Christ—Example. 3. Privacy.
4. Self-esteem—Religious aspects—Christianity. 5. Vocation—Christianity. I. Title.
BT303.C55 2006
232.92'7—dc22   2006002423

Printed in the United States of America
11 12 13 QG 10 9 8 7 6

contents

prologue
in winter

He is like a tree planted by streams of water,
which yields its fruit in season.
—Psalm 1:3

A century ago, a few fragile seeds fell upon rocky soil. Through drought and flood, they clung tightly to earth, stubbornly stretching toward the heavens. Today, silver maple, post oak, and black walnut trees surround our home like tall, loyal sentinels. Their intricate, mingled root systems support the ground below. Their long, angular boughs weave a canopy above. Before I was, they were. My elders by many decades, their presence is steadying.

In the heat, I rest under the covering of their rich foliage. Bursting with shades of green, the leaves dance in the breeze. Winter's reduction is coming, but that does not halt the dance. Trees celebrate the moment, temporary though it is. In the spring, their new growth sings of hope. Their lush greenery offers peace in the summer. In the fall, their colorful collages inspire creativity. And in their emptiness, trees grace the winter with silent elegance.

Though my skin prefers their role in summer, somehow my soul prefers their lessons in winter. Then, when growth pauses, the trees have often become my teachers.

What the plenty of summer hides, the nakedness of winter reveals: infrastructure. Fullness often distracts from foundations. But in the stillness of winter, the trees' true strength is unveiled. Stripped of decoration, the tree trunks become prominent.

As a child I always colored tree trunks brown, but to my adult eyes they appear to be more of a warm gray. Starting with their thick bases, I begin studying each tree. Buckling strips of bark clothe mile after mile of weathered branches. Leafless, the trees feature their intricate support systems. Detail is visible, as is dead wood. Lifeless limbs concealed by summer's boasting are now exposed.

My eyes glide from one rough, uneven bough to another and then to the terminal, delicate twigs. A tree's posture is all-open, like arms ready for an embrace. So very vulnerable, yet so very strong. I find the display quieting and full of grace.

In winter, are the trees bare? Yes.
In winter, are the trees barren? No.

Life still is.

Life does not sleep—though in winter she retracts all advertisement. And when she does so, she is conserving and preparing for the future.

And so it is with us. Seasonally, we too are stripped of visible fruit. Our giftings are hidden; our abilities are underestimated. When previous successes fade and current efforts falter, we can easily mistake our fruitlessness for failure.

But such is the rhythm of spiritual life: new growth, fruit-fulness, transition, rest . . . new growth, fruitfulness, transition, rest. Abundance may make us feel more productive, but perhaps emptiness has greater power to strengthen our souls.

In spiritual winters, our fullness is thinned so that, undis-tracted by our giftings, we can focus upon our character. In the absence of anything to measure, we are left with nothing to stare at except for our foundation.

Risking inspection, we begin to examine the motivations that support our deeds, the attitudes that influence our words, the dead wood otherwise hidden beneath our busyness. Then a life-changing transition occurs as we move from resistance through repentance to the place of rest. With gratitude, we simply abide. Like a tree planted by living water, we focus upon our primary responsibility: remaining in him.

In winter are we bare? Yes.
In winter are we barren? No.

True life still is.

The Father's work in us does not sleep—though in spiritual winters he retracts all advertisement. And when he does so, he is purifying our faith, strengthening our character, conserving our energy, and preparing us for the future.

The sleepy days of winter hide us so that seductive days of summer will not ruin us.

PART ONE

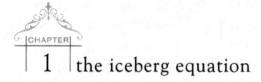

hidden treasure

CHAPTER

1 the iceberg equation

Have you ever felt hidden?

Have you ever moved to a new place or entered a new environment where no one knew who you were, what you could do, or what dreams ignited your soul?

Have you ever crossed the threshold into another season of life, like parenthood or extended studies, where you shifted from recognition to anonymity, from the court to the bench, from standing as a leader to sitting as a learner again?

Have you ever resigned or retired from a position or title and transitioned from being sought out to left out, consulted to unconsidered, celebrated to celebrating others?

In these hidden seasons, we are more familiar with being invisible than acclaimed. Concealed for months or years or decades, our potential seems to hibernate like a bear in winter, and over time we begin to wonder if spring will ever awaken it again.

Hidden hopes. Hidden dreams. Hidden gifts. All of us are acquainted with chapters in life when our visible fruitfulness is

pruned back, our previously praiseworthy strengths become dor-
mant, and our abilities are unnoticed by the watching world.
Like a flower whose budding glory is covered up by wet leaves,
we sense the weight of hiddenness in our hearts and whisper, "I
have so much more to give and be."

But there is One who can see the beauty of that covered,
smothered flower: God himself. And, mysteriously, his delight
in that beauty is not diminished by its leafy camouflage. Neither
would his pleasure be amplified by the flower's visibility. Good
news indeed for the hidden.

In fact, obedience to this God who appreciates the visible and
invisible equally has led many truly great souls into long seasons of anonymity. Some emerged from obscurity into eminence.
Others remained relatively unknown. All agreed that God never
wastes anyone's time.

Whether we enter hiddenness deliberately (as in pursuing an
education or relocating with a new job) or unwillingly (as in an
extended illness or in grief following the loss of a loved one), we
can spend years feeling that the greatest part of us is submerged
in the unseen, as though others can only see the tip of the iceberg of who we really are.

Through chattering teeth, arctic scientists inform us that only
one-eighth to one-tenth of an iceberg is visible. As much as 90
percent is submerged in the unseen. Because of their enormous
mass, with that proportion, icebergs are virtually indestructible.

10% visible + 90% unseen = an indestructible life

The most influential life in all of history reflected the iceberg equation. Ninety percent of his life on earth was spent in obscurity. Ten percent of his earthly life was spent in the public eye. And all of his life was, and still is, absolutely indestructible.

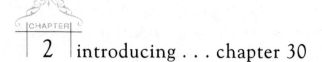

2 | introducing . . . chapter 30

Of the Gospels' eighty-nine total chapters, only four offer any information about Jesus' life before the beginning of his public ministry. Mark and John skip the subject entirely. From this fraction of information about Jesus' early life provided in the Gospels of Matthew and Luke, we glean the following:

- ✢ Jesus was born in Bethlehem in a smelly animal pen (followed by hidden days).
- ✢ He was circumcised in the temple on his eighth day (followed by hidden months).
- ✢ Before turning two, Jesus received a visit from Eastern wise men (followed by hidden years).
- ✢ At the age of twelve, Jesus got in trouble for staying in the temple, listening and asking questions when he was supposed to be with his parents' family headed back home (followed by almost two entirely hidden decades).

Eighteen years after the temple incident, Jesus emerged from hiddenness, and his adult ministry commenced by the Jordan River at a wild man's baptismal service! All four writers of the Gospels mark the beginning of Jesus' earthly ministry by introducing John the Baptist and his declarations concerning Jesus:

> *The people were waiting expectantly and were all*
> *wondering in their hearts if John might possibly*

be the Christ. John answered them all, "I baptize you with water. But one more powerful than I will come, the thongs of whose sandals I am not worthy to untie. He will baptize you with the Holy Spirit and with fire. His winnowing fork is in his hand to clear his threshing floor and to gather the wheat into his barn, but he will burn up the chaff with unquenchable fire." ❧ (Luke 3:15–17; see also Matthew 3:11 and Mark 1:7–8)

The next day John saw Jesus coming toward him and said, "Look, the Lamb of God, who takes away the sin of the world! This is the one I meant when I said, 'A man who comes after me has surpassed me because he was before me.' I myself did not know him, but the reason I came baptizing with water was that he might be revealed to Israel." ❧ (John 1:29–31)

A powerful (and slightly frightening) introduction! But it is important for us to remember that this starting point marked by the Gospel writers is not chapter 1 of Jesus' life; it is chapter 30. We know practically nothing about Jesus' first 29 hidden chapters of life. Only three years, less than 10 percent, of Jesus' days are visible through the writings of the Bible. Over 90 percent of his earthly life is submerged in the unseen.

However, when we state our desire to "be like Jesus," we are not referring to Jesus' anonymous years. "I want to walk like Jesus walked and live like Jesus lived!" is generally *not* equated in our hearts with, "I want to live 90 percent of my life in absolute obscurity!"

Our enthusiastic declarations that we want to "be like Jesus" reference Jesus' visible years . . . with a few notable exceptions. In these statements we are *not* saying, "I want to subject my body, spirit, and mind to an extended wilderness experience," or, "I want to be brutally beaten, suffer excruciating pain, and be murdered at the hands of mocking sinners."

No. Our desire to "be like Jesus" contains several exemption clauses, not the least of which are Jesus' hidden years, desert experiences, temptations, tortures, and crucifixion. We will pass on those, thank you. What we *are* most definitely interested in, however, is Jesus' character and authority. How we long to see his character and authority transform this broken world through our lives!

But Jesus' character and authority are not isolated entities. They are not disconnected commodities we can purchase at a discount. Jesus' character and authority come with Jesus' life, 90 percent of which was lived in quiet anonymity.

"What would Jesus do?" we ask sincerely (in word and song, on T-shirts and in bracelets). Well, for starters, he embraced a life of hiddenness. As we will soon see, Jesus' hidden years empowered him to live an eternally fruitful life.

3 | quite literally formative

hid•den \hi-dᵊn\ *adjective* 1 : being out of sight or not readily apparent : CONCEALED 2 : OBSCURE, UNEXPLAINED, UNDISCLOSED[1]

Who would wrap a flawless, exquisitely cut, utterly unique diamond in common newspaper? From the accounts of Jesus' life, it appears that God would! He offers to humanity his Son—the most pure, precious, and priceless of gifts—wrapped in plain, nondescript paper. Then, along with the angels, it seems as though God watches history unfold like a parent with anticipation thinking, *I can't wait for them to realize what I've given them inside that package!*

So Father God clothes his Son with human flesh, hosts the birth of the world's Savior in a stable, and dispatches an elite angelic company to make the announcement of all ages before a small, somewhat less than internationally influential band of shepherds.

This was unexpected even by the devout. Diamonds are supposed to be displayed dramatically, not hidden discretely. All along, the people thought their promised Messiah would appear in convincing power to lead them spiritually and politically into a new day. They thought the packaging would be removed in a spectacular fashion before their eyes. Who would have guessed that God in his wisdom would conceal his gift for thirty years and then plan for the last shreds of packaging to be removed and the greatness of his Son to be fully revealed only in death?

Hence, this word *hidden* characterizes the vast majority of Jesus' life on earth. Why? Why would Father God wrap the glory of heaven in plain paper, announce the birth of his precious Gift with a full angelic choir, and then hide this priceless package for three decades?

We certainly would not have permitted the Son of God to live in anonymity for 90 percent of his life! Every breath would have been monitored by the brightest minds in medical research. Every movement would have been captured by the media and analyzed by psychologists. Every word would have been weighed by theologians, recorded by historians, and printed on tastefully designed posters.

Hidden? No way! Our tendency is to only hide things that are shameful or incomplete or insignificant. So when we see the gaps in Jesus' story we are apt to think, *Too bad. I would have liked to know more. But I am glad that the biblical writers documented the most important moments of Jesus' life.*

Now, certainly all that is recorded in the Scriptures about Jesus' life on earth is eternally essential and valuable. But does it then follow that the unrecorded is unessential or of lesser value? Because we naturally grant more weight to the visible than the invisible, it is easy for us to underestimate the vital importance of the three undocumented decades preceding Jesus' three cele-brated years of public ministry.

However, with his life (and with ours), it is critical that we not mistake *unseen* for *unimportant.*

Consider human conception. Life commences in the dark warmth of the womb. God knits us together there with infinitely creative hands concealing from our curiosity his most mysterious act of creation. Unseen? Yes. Unimportant? Not remotely. These months in the womb are quite literally formative. When this hidden phase of development is prematurely interrupted, the results can be tragic.

Or consider the growth of a plant. Before a gardener can enjoy a plant's fruit, she must tenderly and strategically attend to its root. So a plant's birth begins with its burial. The gardener commits a generally unremarkable seed to the silence of the soil, where it sits in stillness and lightlessness, hidden by the smothering dirt. Just when it appears as though death is imminent, its seeming decay reveals new life. The seed becomes less and yet more of its former self, and in that transformation takes hold of the darkness and reaches for the sun. All that is to come rests greatly upon the plant's ability to tightly and sightlessly develop roots in unseen places.

As with a child in the womb and a seed in the ground, God's unanticipated move of hiding Jesus granted him protected, undisturbed room to be and become. From God's perspective, anonymous seasons are sacred spaces. They are quite literally formative; to be rested in, not rushed through—and most definitely never to be regretted.

Unapplauded, but not unproductive: hidden years are the surprising birthplace of true spiritual greatness.

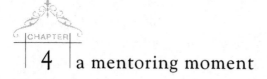

4 | a mentoring moment

Allow me to explain how the book you hold in your hands emerged. Years ago, I was prayerfully preparing a teaching. As usual, God did not tell me what to say. He simply inclined my heart in the direction of what I needed to study. That inclination led me to restudy passages from the Bible that describe the temptation of Jesus.

Previously, I had viewed Jesus' temptation as a real trial in his present and a foreshadowing of the trials he would face in his future as he walked toward the cross. Turning to the passages this time, I found myself remembering a decade-old conversation with one of my first mentors, whom I will call Marie.

Marie was a very private person, but when she opened the door to her personal life you needed to take notes. I always called her with a journal open and a pen poised. This woman was profound. And like most truly profound people, she was intimately familiar with pain. One day, Marie told me about a friend who visited her in the hospital after her third miscarriage. Trying to console her, the well-meaning friend had said, "You know, Marie, God is going to make you even stronger through this."

My mentor smiled, thanked her friend, and thought about her words for several days. Relaying the hospital conversation to me, Marie explained that though she appreciated her friend's intention, she questioned her friend's conclusion about the purpose of pain. Marie ended our time together that day with this thought: "I feel that trials do not prepare us for what's to come as much as they reveal what we've done with our lives up to this point."

As Marie considered the pain of her third miscarriage, she realized that her response to this trial was less of a window into her future than it was a window into her past. Her current choices reflected and revealed her past choices. How had she responded previously when her dearest dreams perished in her womb? Did she withdraw from God in bitterness or come near to him with her unanswered questions? Had she tried to outrun the pain, or had she given herself permission to grieve and let the tears wash her wounds? The choices of her yesterdays were revealed through the window of her responses to her current trial.

In other words, trials tell us less about our future than they do about our past. Why? Because the decisions we make in difficult places today are greatly the product of decisions we made in the unseen places of our yesterdays.

5 | through the window

Meditating on Marie's experience, a principle began forming in my mind: today's decisions foreshadow tomorrow's challenges and reflect yesterday's choices.

For example, let us say that Kevin made unapplauded choices in his twenties and thirties to exercise fairly regularly and eat healthy foods. He never appeared on the cover of a nutrition magazine, nor was he featured in the "heroes for today" section of the local newspaper. He simply woke up each morning and consistently chose to exercise and eat well. His friend Doug also made simple, consistent, unapplauded choices regarding exercise and diet through passive postponement, i.e., "I'll work on that later." "Later," however, did not make its debut until Doug turned forty and began experiencing the unfortunate realities of what I call genetic displacement.

Question: Both Kevin and Doug are facing increased poundage, but whose past choices incline him to make healthy decisions today? Exactly. Kevin's past choices have clustered over the years and created momentum toward healthier living. So is poor Doug doomed to eventually look like Great (and I do mean "great" in every sense of the word) Uncle Alfred? No. But the momentum of his past choices will create resistance as Doug tries to head in a new, healthier direction for his second half of life.

Rather discouraging for Doug, some may note. Perhaps, but it is reality. And, frankly, I would rather have the truth than an illusion, regardless of how temporarily encouraging that illusion may appear. For both Kevin and Doug, this is not chapter 1 of their lives; it is chapter 40. For better or for worse, the decisions they currently are facing reflect the choices they previously have made.

Let us reconsider my mentor's quote: "I feel that trials do not prepare us for what's to come as much as they reveal what we've done with our lives up to this point." With Marie's wisdom in my soul, I turned once again to the passages that recorded Jesus' wilderness experience. Suddenly I realized that these first steps in Jesus' public ministry actually opened a window into Jesus' unseen past! For Jesus, and for us, "today" does not exist in a vacuum. Each day is in some way shaped by the days preceding it and in turn has an effect upon the days following it.

By examining the decisions Jesus made in chapter 30 of his life, we gain insight into Father God's formative work in Jesus during chapters 1 through 29! His baptism and wilderness experience hold significance, not only for his present and future, but also for his past. Because the strongest influences on the decisions Jesus made *in* the desert were the choices he had been making *before* the desert. In hidden places over hidden years, Jesus' choices clustered and created momentum that is revealed through the decisions he made in his public ministry.

Jesus' first three decades were mostly unrecorded, but they were not uneventful. By examining the first decisions and experiences of Jesus in his celebrated, public ministry we will begin to recognize the riches Father God planted in him (and seeks to plant in us) in anonymous, uncelebrated seasons of hiddenness.

6 reflections

At the end of each part in *anonymous*, you will find an
informal chapter such as this one that contains a set
of personal reflections. God connects with each of us
uniquely. Personally, I seem to interact most intimately
with him outside on a quiet stroll or in my prayer room
while playing the piano, meditating on the Scriptures,
or thinking with pen and paper in hand. Though I would
prefer to talk and walk with you through our dry creek
bed, in these chapters I invite you to share a few moments
with me and my journal (and hopefully a hot cup of
tea or coffee!). These pages contain raw reflections and
personal struggles with the destiny-determining choices
we all face in anonymous seasons.

*Some struggle with living in the past, others with living for
the moment. Personally, my struggle has more often been in
living for the future. As a young adult, my gaze was always
set toward the next step or season or degree or plan or place
or . . .*

*Distracted with daydreams of tomorrow's potential, I
often found today's reality pale and tasteless in comparison.
Before I could even be capable of valuing hidden years, I first
had to start valuing each day as something more than just a
boring prelude to the exciting future.*

My perspective is thankfully different now (one or two or twenty-something years later), and I trace the beginnings of that shift to an unusual experience around a dinner table. After finishing my undergraduate studies, I went to Asia and eventually found myself tutoring students in English at a church-sponsored study hall on Tsing Yi Island. The beautiful people and their fascinating culture completely captivated me. In fact, I planned to spend my entire life serving and learning from the Chinese. (Obviously, since I am writing from the Ozarks of Missouri, that plan has since been revised.)

While there, my co-workers invited me to a "banquet," which I equated in my mind with eating lots of food plus meeting lots of people plus enduring a painfully constructed speech. Walking into the restaurant, I soon discovered that Chinese banquets are more like journeys than meals. The experience that night unfolded slowly over several hours as course after course of what ultimately became a twelve-course meal was presented at our large, round, rotating table.

Back home in Texas, normally the first "course" at a restaurant was a bright bowl of chips and salsa. Of Hispanic descent, I genetically craved good salsa, but that is not why I went to restaurants. The chips and salsa were just fillers —something to get past, to get through, to get on with the main course that was not there yet (but was coming!). Then perhaps course number two would be a salad. Most often it was quite clear that the master chef had not touched that salad. It too was just a filler, something to get past, to get through, to get on with the main course that was not there yet (but was coming!).

Well, something surprised me about that Chinese banquet. Through course after course after course, I was not able to identify anything as "just a filler." Nothing stood out as "only an appetizer" to get through, to get past, to get on with the main course that was not there yet (but was coming!). Every course—in presentation, in taste, in texture—bore the marks of a master chef. Then the obvious occurred to me: the reason no course looked like a filler was because, from the master chef's perspective, no course was a filler. To him, every course was main.

Now, I confess that after a while I became a little distracted at the banquet and my mind started wandering back to past courses. Like that shark-fin soup—what was I thinking? Why did I not get more of that dish when I had the chance?! Then my thoughts would drift ahead to future courses as I worried about the possibility of chicken feet being on the menu. While I spent my energy reminiscing about and regretting the past, or daydreaming about and dreading the future, the course before me grew cold, and I wondered why it did not taste as good as it should.

That experience has returned to my memory countless times because I, and perhaps we, have a tendency to think that "main" is out there, not right here. Main is on hold, waiting to appear until after . . . we finish our education or get married or find that dream job or start a family or resolve that conflict or complete that task or get out of debt or retire or slow down or . . .

In moments when I am tempted to treat this gift called time as though it were some unfortunate filler, I hear a gentle whisper from God in my soul: "Child, I am the God who wastes no man's time. To me, every course in your life is main."

Main is not behind us. Nor is main way out ahead of us. To our God, this course—call it transition, further studies, unexpected illness, financial crisis, grief, or a desert—is as full of potential as any course ever has been and any course ever will be.

Every course—and certainly every day—is a gift from God. (Enjoy it while it's hot.)

PART TWO

from nazareth, with love

CHAPTER

7 | roots

> *"Nazareth! Can anything good come from there?"*
> *Nathanael asked.*
> —John 1:46

If you asked devout Judean Jews in Jesus' day what they thought of Nazareth, you would probably receive a collection of less than favorable adjectives including *small, insignificant, scorned,* and *spiritually suspect.* Nazareth certainly was not the town of kings and prophets. In fact, whereas Jerusalem is mentioned more than 650 times in the Old Testament alone, Nazareth entirely escapes the attention of all biblical writers until the New Testament.

Yet this is where God sent his Son for his first three hidden decades of life. Nestled around the hill, Nazareth slept peacefully between the Sea of Galilee and the Mediterranean. The agricultural community was filled with fewer than two thousand souls and was situated just outside the traffic-laden trade route from Damascus to Egypt, the *Via Maris.*

Nazareth itself was a southern town of Galilee, an economically thriving district under Roman rule. Growing up in this region, Jesus would have become familiar with trade and commerce, farming and fishing, Greek and Roman thought, and a rich variety of languages. Most today would value such a multicultural environment, but some crinkled their noses at the mention of Galilee. They felt Galilean Jews were too tolerant of non-Jewish cultures and practices.

Tolerance is a rather complex concept. Though it was true that Galileans were more exposed to a diversity of beliefs and peoples, most would hesitate to equate exposure to difference with the dilution of doctrine. Nonetheless, more than a few southern Jews were certain that this exposure had contaminated the purity of their northern cousins' faith. Later, even when they were eyewitnesses to Jesus' miracles, the Jews in Jerusalem would spiritually stumble over his boyhood roots in Galilee:

> On hearing his words, some of the people said, "Surely this man is the Prophet." Others said, "He is the Christ." Still others asked, "How can the Christ come from Galilee? Does not the Scripture say that the Christ will come from David's family and from Bethlehem, the town where David lived?"
> ❧ (John 7:40–42)

The citizens of Nazareth no doubt held at least a slightly higher opinion of Galilee, but even they did not expect a prophet to come from Jesus' family. Paging back in our memories, we may be able to recall former classmates who were voted "most likely to succeed." They demonstrated some special ability or unique gifting or annoyingly consistent excellence that made them seem destined for greatness. Evidently the good folks in Nazareth never nominated Jesus for this award.

During his public years of ministry when Jesus returned to his hometown and taught in the synagogue, the people were stunned. But their response was not, "That's our boy!" or, "Always knew he was special!" or, "We saw it in him long ago!" Throughout almost three decades it had never occurred to this small community that Jesus might be made of prophetic (let alone messianic) material. In response to Jesus' amazing ministry, they said:

> *"Where did this man get this wisdom and these miraculous powers?" they asked. "Isn't this the carpenter's son? Isn't his mother's name Mary, and aren't his brothers James, Joseph, Simon and Judas? Aren't all his sisters with us? Where then did this man get all these things?" And they took offense at him.* ✥ (Matthew 13:54–57)

So Jesus grew up as a relatively un-celebrated boy from an un-royal family in the un-respected town of an un-liked region. Bad news if you are planning on running for office; good news if your job description is embracing hiddenness. Frustrating if you crave notoriety; freeing if you value learning without paparazzi.

8 | a delayed destiny

Somewhere, somehow in the thick of those long, undocumented years, Jesus awakened to his divine nature and calling. He realized and accepted that he was the Son of God, eternally existent as God and yet temporally present as a man. More than a prophet and more than a king, Jesus was with God in the beginning, created all that is, and was now on earth to offer his sinless life as a sacrifice for our sins.

Were it not true, such a belief would be the height of delusion. But the deluded do not act as Jesus acted. They wear their assumptions clumsily, greedily, and loudly. Not so with Jesus. He was comfortably clothed in the supreme mystery of the Incarnation. He wore his divine power with humility and grace.

Every day following this awakening Jesus would have wondered, *Is today the day?* Imagine Jesus, with God's divine power and calling breathing and bursting within him, waking up each morning, turning to Father God in prayer and asking, "Are we there yet?!" Day after day, month after month, and year after year Father God simply replied, "No, my Son. We are not there yet. Today is not the day."

Now place that private reality side by side with Jesus' public reality. Picture Jesus—still with God's divine power and calling breathing and bursting within him—waking up each morning and walking throughout his town and region. Most folks would probably not even notice him (after all, he was an un-celebrated boy from an un-royal family). Some might possibly even scorn him (because of his roots or the rumors that may have surrounded his conception). And all would definitely underestimate him. (How could they do otherwise?!)

What a combination! During these uncelebrated years, Jesus submitted to a seemingly delayed destiny. A God-sized mission pulsated in his heart, but he was not free to explain it, proclaim it, or actively pursue it. Onlookers saw only the tip of the iceberg of who Jesus truly was, and they could have never imagined the indestructible greatness growing just beneath the surface of Jesus' unapplauded life.

What would that experience build in someone?

What does it build *in us*? What grows in that underestimated gap between God's calling and others' perceptions, between our true capabilities and our current realities? Most of us struggle if our dreams are delayed one year, let alone twenty! We find God's pauses perplexing. They seem to be a waste of our potential. When those pauses extend beyond what we can comprehend or explain (say, for instance, three days), we often spiral into self-doubt or second-guessing.

But in anonymous seasons we must hold tightly to the truth that no doubt strengthened Jesus throughout his hidden years: Father God is neither *care*-less nor *cause*-less with how he spends our lives. When he calls a soul simultaneously to greatness and obscurity, the fruit—if we wait for it—can change the world.

9 | it is time!

Then Jesus came from Galilee to the Jordan
to be baptized by John.
—Matthew 3:13

Finally, after years of disciplined waiting, Father God has an unusual answer for Jesus' usual question:

"So . . . are we there yet, Father?" a grinning Jesus might have
offered as he concluded his morning prayers and turned to walk
to work.

"Actually, we are," replied Father God with a curious ache
softening his normally strong voice.

(silence)

"We are? We are . . . there?!" Jesus asked in rising anticipation.

"In a word: yes. Today is the day, Son. Leave your tools on
the table. I've made an appointment for you with a holy man in
camel's hair."

There.

Where is *there* for you? What does it look like? What do you
think it will feel like? *There*, for Jesus, was a miraculous but mis-
understood journey toward a splintered, bloody cross.

Leaving his hometown, Jesus' steps must have been filled with thought. He apparently traveled alone those thirty to sixty miles from Nazareth to somewhere along the Jordan River. Historically, he walked from the scorned to the significant. Spiritually, he journeyed from anonymity into global renown.

On the other side he would encounter Cousin John, an odd but strangely endearing, organic fellow. Diplomacy was not at the center of John's gifting cluster, but sincere souls by the hundreds were drawn to his raw, unedited call to repentance.

> *In those days John the Baptist came, preaching*
> *in the Desert of Judea and saying, "Repent, for*
> *the kingdom of heaven is near." . . . People went*
> *out to him from Jerusalem and all Judea and the*
> *whole region of the Jordan. Confessing their sins,*
> *they were baptized by him in the Jordan River.* ❧
> (Matthew 3:1–2, 5–6)

Ceremonial cleansing was a familiar concept in John's day. Those desiring to embrace the Jewish faith fulfilled several obligations including a "ritual bath to wash away the impurities" of their pagan past.[1] However, John proclaimed a baptism of repentance for those already committed to—not merely converting to—faith in God.

This was slightly scandalous. John challenged his hearers to take personal responsibility for their sins and not rely smugly on their ancestry for acceptance in God's sight. When people responded to John's message and stepped into the Jordan, they were saying, "I have sinned. May God forgive me. May he strengthen me to follow him in holiness and prepare me to receive the

Messiah he has promised to send."

What the people did not know was that their long-awaited Messiah had also been waiting! He was alive and well, living in quiet anonymity in the unlikely town of Nazareth.

Imagine how Jesus must have felt when he arrived at the Jordan, saw the crowds of mostly sincere souls, and heard John yell out, "Prepare the way for the Lord, make straight paths for him" (Luke 3:4). In response, most of us would have exploded with tearful emotion, "HERE I AM. I HAVE FINALLY COME. GOD SENT ME TO BRING YOU NEW LIFE!"

But not Jesus. Instead, he calmly navigated his way through the people and waded into the Jordan toward John. And all the people gasped and thought, *There he is! There's our long-awaited Messiah!* Doubtful. My guess is that they were all thinking, *There's one more repentant sinner. I think that makes at least fifty-two today.*

No parade. No drum roll. Not even an explanation. Jesus allowed himself to be thought of as a sinner. Only John knew the truth about the sinless One standing before him:

> But John tried to deter him, saying, "I need to be baptized by you, and do you come to me?" Jesus replied, "Let it be so now; it is proper for us to do this to fulfill all righteousness." Then John consented.
> ॐ (Matthew 3:14–15)

How could he do that? Especially after waiting for decades in anonymity, how could he not immediately let the people know who he really was and all that was in his heart?

Jesus' anonymous season had prepared him for this moment. The choices he made *in* the Jordan River are reflections of choices he had been making *before* the Jordan River. Something in surrendering to hiddenness strengthened Jesus to not make a name for himself, to not be his own PR person. Something in embracing that prolonged season of obscurity enabled him to appear to be less in order to be able to do more.

Hidden years, when heeded, empower a soul to patiently trust God with their press releases. All that waiting actually grants us the strength to wait a little longer and not rush God's plans for our lives.

CHAPTER

10 reflections

Throughout Jesus' hidden years, he demonstrated one of the great forgotten virtues of our time: patience. But how can we practically follow Jesus' example and be patient when God-size dreams pound in our souls? Seasonally, this struggle has been agonizing. On the one hand, I am inundated with messages imploring me to package and market the dream quickly, efficiently, and strategically before it is too late. On the other hand, fear of failure and rejection paralyzes me so that by default I assume a posture of noncooperation with God's plans.

But there is quite a bit of room between self-promotion and utter passivity in our stewardship of God-size dreams. At present, I am attempting to rest in alert availability. "Alert" because I am not living in denial of the dreams in my heart. "Available" because God is a gentleman and I am quite comfortable waiting for him to open doors. Truth is, I do not have enough character to walk through doors I open for myself.

I liken God's purposes to a pure but unpredictable river. Impatient self-promotion actively seeks out a speedboat to outrun the current and rush toward the future. Fear of failure stands on the banks cautiously to observe before even getting her feet wet. But perhaps obedience simply wades into the center and lets the current of God's presence set the pace, be it swift or still.

Because, after all, is not our true aim and aspiration just to be near God? Jesus seems to exemplify this perspective. Whether "Not yet, my Son" tucked him away in obscurity or "Now is the time" made him the news, Jesus appears to have walked unstressed and unhurried. His peaceful pace seems to imply that he measured himself not by where he was going and how fast he could get there but by whom he was following and how closely they walked together.

Patience grows well in such soil. She is the ally of a soul that makes God its primary pursuit, because in this journey called life, regardless of the scenery, such a soul is deeply contented in the Company.

PART THREE

out of anonymity

CHAPTER

11 | a split sky

Day one: a holy birth . . . then hidden days

Day eight: a baby dedication . . . then hidden months

Year two: a visit from wise men . . . then hidden years

Year twelve: a time in the temple . . . then almost two entirely hidden decades

At the age of thirty, long years of silence are shattered as a relatively unknown Jesus steps into the Jordan River to be baptized by John.

> *As Jesus was coming up out of the water, he saw*
> *heaven being torn open and the Spirit descending*
> *on him like a dove.* ❧ (Mark 1:10)

John's calloused, cracked hands guided a willing Jesus under the cool waters of the Jordan. The baptism only lasted a moment, but John had been waiting a lifetime for that moment. His God-size dream was to prepare the way for the Messiah, and he had risked all to fulfill God's call. Now, looking into Jesus' face under the clear waters, John realized with relief-filled joy that God's chosen One had come. Jesus' time was beginning, and his own was fading. What happened next certainly fortified John's faith for the disillusioning days to come.

With a prayer in his heart, Jesus broke through the surface and came up out of the Jordan. Just as the water began to bead off of his face, the sky ripped open like a cloth being torn in two. Looking up, John and Jesus saw the Holy Spirit descending from that tear in the heavens "in bodily form like a dove" (Luke 3:22). Reflecting on the experience, John would later add the following:

> *I saw the Spirit come down from heaven as a dove and remain on him. I would not have known him, except that the one who sent me to baptize with water told me, "The man on whom you see the Spirit come down and remain is he who will baptize with the Holy Spirit." I have seen and I testify that this is the Son of God.* ❧ (John 1:32–34)

Imagine!

The Holy Spirit, being God and all, could have taken any form he pleased. Something with wings certainly helps when one is planning on descending from heaven, but he could have chosen to come as an eagle or an albatross or even a sparrow. But he chose a dove, once again as after the Genesis flood, symbolic of a new day on this old earth of ours. (See Genesis 8:10–12.)[1]

From the writings of the Gospels, we do not know if everyone else at the Jordan River saw the sky split apart and the Holy Spirit gracefully descend as a dove upon Jesus. Perhaps they were as awestruck as John the Baptist was, or perhaps they were simply grateful for a break in the clouds. Maybe they were baffled by Jesus' and John's intense peering into the heavens, or maybe they sat there wondering about the guy with the bird on his shoulder (that would be hard to miss).

But regardless of what the crowds thought, the experience was unmistakably prophetic to John and Jesus. They would have immediately recalled the treasured words of hope spoken some seven centuries earlier about the year of God's favor:

> The Spirit of the Sovereign LORD is on me,
>   because the LORD has anointed me
>   to preach good news to the poor.
> He has sent me to bind up the brokenhearted,
>   to proclaim freedom for the captives
>   and release from darkness for the prisoners,
> to proclaim the year of the LORD's favor
>   and the day of vengeance of our God,
> to comfort all who mourn,
>   and provide for those who grieve in Zion—
> to bestow on them a crown of beauty
>   instead of ashes,

the oil of gladness
   instead of mourning,
and a garment of praise
   instead of a spirit of despair. ❧ (Isaiah 61:1–3)

Good news. Freedom. Release. Favor. Vengeance. Comfort. Provision. Beauty. Gladness. Praise. As the Spirit descended like a dove upon Jesus, these images of transformation—affecting individual lives and the fabric of entire communities—flooded John's and Jesus' minds. But God was not finished yet.

The curtains were drawn. The blessing had been given. Now Father God had something he wanted to say.

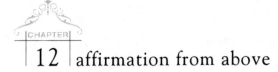

12 affirmation from above

Perhaps you, like me, have never heard an audible voice from God. But if you could, what would you want him to say?

Would you hope for him to offer an explanation? ("Your loved one died because . . .") Or would you desire an answer to a burning prayer? ("Yes, that is *the one*.") Would you prefer direction or guidance? ("My child, invest thou in soybeans.") Or insight into the future? ("The pain will go away August 23 at the stroke of noon.") If your ears were going to hear God's voice only once, what words would you long for him to speak?

Jesus and John could certainly have benefited from all of the above. But evidently there was something they both needed to hear more than explanations of the past or foretelling of the future:

> And a voice from heaven said, "This is my Son,
> whom I love; with him I am well pleased." ❧
> (Matthew 3:17)

From the open heavens, Jesus and John heard an audible sound—the living *voice* of God. Though other writers use this word to speak of *rumblings* of thunder and the *roar* of many waters, Matthew's usage does not indicate whether God's voice sounded that day with great volume or in hushed tones.[1] But considering the river and the crowds and the distance, we can safely assume that God was not whispering. Surely his voice that day was deep, full, and forceful like an ocean—resonating throughout their whole beings.

Father God's pronouncement contained three essential elements. First, he acknowledged Jesus as his Son.

Odds are that we are culturally immune to the startling claim carried in these words. "Son of God" was clearly a messianic image for the devout of Jesus' day. Additionally, in Jesus' culture, to boldly identify yourself as God's Son was to make yourself equal with God. So if there is only one God and you claim to be his equal, then you are actually claiming to be him!

Occasionally, sincere (and a handful of not-so-sincere) folks suggest that Jesus never professed to be God. But in order for me to believe that Jesus never claimed to be God, I would have to—for integrity's sake—simultaneously rip a few hundred pages out of my Bible. In his cultural and religious context, Jesus so clearly claimed to be God that the spiritual leaders accused him of blasphemy:

> *Jesus said to them, "My Father is always at his work to this very day, and I, too, am working." For this reason the Jews tried all the harder to kill him; not only was he breaking the Sabbath, but he was even calling God his own Father, making himself equal with God.* (John 5:17–18)

> *Again the Jews picked up stones to stone him, but Jesus said to them, "I have shown you many great miracles from the Father. For which of these do you stone me?" "We are not stoning you for any*

of these," replied the Jews, "but for blasphemy,
because you, a mere man, claim to be God." ❧
(John 10:31–33)

Jesus answered them, . . . "Why then do you accuse
me of blasphemy because I said, 'I am God's Son'?
Do not believe me unless I do what my Father
does. But if I do it, even though you do not believe
me, believe the miracles, that you may know and
understand that the Father is in me, and I in the
Father." ❧ (John 10:34, 36–38)

Was Jesus fully man? Yes. Was Jesus fully God? Yes. We call that
a mystery—one that Father God shouted from the heavens and
Jesus echoed on earth.

Having fully captivated Jesus' and John's attention, of all the
things Father God could have said, his first words were neither
directional ("Go here") nor instructional ("Do this"). They were
relational: "This is my Son."

13 | before

Following his declaration of relationship *with* Jesus, Father God next affirms his commitment *to* Jesus:

> *This is my Son, whom I love.* ❧ (Matthew 3:17)

The word here translated *love* is more often rendered *dear friend(s)* because it carries a sense of tenderly treasured friendship. In this second element of God's thundered sentence, he explains that—in addition to being his Son—Jesus is also his beloved friend whom he treasures with tenderness.

The first element was relational and the second committal. The third speaks of God's approval over Jesus' life:

> *This is my Son, whom I love; with him I am well pleased.* ❧ (Matthew 3:17)

Well pleased comes to us from a Greek word that combines a prefix meaning "well" or "good" with a verb that means "to consider, believe, or suppose." In various translations, it can be rendered "enjoy, be pleased with, take pleasure, think good of," and "delight." This phrase—"with him I am well pleased"—communicates the emotional pleasure the Father had in the Son.

How might Jesus have felt, hearing such words? After long years of waiting and wondering, after decades of anonymously stewarding God's global cause and call in his soul, the heavens finally parted, and God said, "You are my Child! Know that I deeply love you and tenderly treasure you. Rest assured that I am so very delighted in who you are!"

We have no way of knowing how often Father God echoed these words privately to Jesus. But we do know of at least one other time where he sounded them from the heavens:

> *Jesus took with him Peter, James and John the brother of James, and led them up a high mountain by themselves. There he was transfigured before them. His face shone like the sun, and his clothes became as white as the light. Just then there appeared before them Moses and Elijah, talking with Jesus. . . . [A] bright cloud enveloped them, and a voice from the cloud said, "This is my Son, whom I love; with him I am well pleased. Listen to him!"*
> ❧ (Matthew 17:1–3, 5)

These sky-splitting affirmations bookend Jesus' public ministry. He hears Father God's trio of relationship, commitment, and approval toward the beginning in a river valley and toward the end on a mountaintop.

Dick Schroeder, a wise teacher and friend, once noted that the first time Jesus heard these words thundered from the heavens, God spoke them *before* Jesus had ever *done* anything for which we call him Savior.

True.

God sounded his affirmation from above over Jesus' life *before* Jesus ever preached one sermon or enlightened one mind, *before* Jesus ever healed one body or saved one soul.

These loving words were spoken over Jesus *before* the timeless teachings, the dramatic deliverances, and the many miracles. They were spoken over his *hidden* years. God declared his full acceptance and pride over what Jesus had become through his *anonymous* season. In unseen places over underestimated years, Jesus had been making unrecorded, unapplauded choices that had prepared him for everything to come. And Father God— who values the seen and unseen alike—was very, very pleased.

Through Jesus, we inherit this trio of God's Fatherhood, love, and acceptance. We inherit *the affirmation from above*, for God is still shouting these words of love over his children even *before* we are recognized or celebrated, *before* we make the grade or make the news or even make dinner. *Before* we get that promotion or even get out of bed, Father God is already shouting. Not because of any stunning accomplishment but because of who we are: through Jesus, we are his!

That shout is worthy of a prayerful pause. So take a moment. Allow God's affirmation from above to echo in your soul: "*I love you, my child, my friend. You are my treasure. And I am so very proud of you.*"

Is there anything else in the whole wide world that our souls truly need to hear?

14 reflections

What news! God is pleased with my hidden years. He does not view anonymous seasons as boring and unfortunate preludes to be rushed through quickly so I can move on to some other season that is more productive and exciting.

And though, like any parent, I am sure God finds joy in every season of our lives, it will not surprise me if in the end we learn that he enjoyed our hidden years the most. They seem less cluttered with the glittery stuff that distracts us from his face.

My children are in their hidden years. They are dancing blissfully in almost complete anonymity. With the exception of a few other privileged souls, my husband and I are their primary audience. How we treasure the show!

Our son's belly laugh—if bottled—could further the cause of world peace. His compassion regularly causes my eyes to leak. Jonathan sends every single penny he has to "the poor children because they do not have milk, or bananas, or computers." And it is still very hard for him to understand why all the planet's orphans cannot come live with us in our house. He is concerned for the world, but without apology he adores his mommy! Once when I was in bed looking pretty puny, he came into my room holding a glass. Taking a drink, he then offered the glass to me and said, "Here, Mommy, drink after me so you can catch my healthy."

Our daughter is liquid sunshine. She is brilliant, beautiful, and dramatic! In a moment of complete silence at a solemn ceremony that was being projected on a big screen, Keona shouted, "Look! I'm on TV!" She feels deeply, tells you about it loudly, and gets over it quickly. And by nature, she is a nurturer. Following my unexpected surgery, Keona would daily ask, "Mommy, are you better yet?" and then proceed to comb my hair with her toothbrush and smash gobs of Vaseline between my toes. I will never forget the first time after that surgery when I was able to walk down the stairs on my own. While I sat at the bottom catching my breath, two-year-old Keona came up and asked if she could hold me. Then, with her beautiful arms wrapped around me, she whispered, "Mommy, I am so proud of you."

You did not know about all that, did you? Nope. And that is OK. These moments have taken place during hidden years that only a few hearts have been graced to observe.

As far as the world is concerned, my children are living in anonymity. Jonathan is yet to realize his unusual blend of exceptional abilities. Keona is still unaware of her striking gift of influence. They are currently unable to take a stand against injustice, research cures for cancer, or even tie their own shoes. They are hidden. And they are the delight of our hearts.

My husband and I treasure beyond words our private viewing of Jonathan and Keona's hidden years. Our front-row seats in their lives are priceless. We are their greatest fans, and for the moment, they are not looking for any others. We are enough. How nice it is to be enough.

I wonder if, in my own life, God feels like I believe he is enough.

Soon we will have competition. Soon others will be impressed by Jonathan's genius and dazzled by Keona's inner and outer beauty. Soon my children will have to navigate through praise and applause, criticism and rejection. Soon the room will be filled with flattering admirers and unwelcome detractors.

But my hope is that our presence, and more importantly the presence of Jesus that we keep drawing their attention to, will steady them. We were there before the crowds came, and he will be there after my husband and I and the crowds have to leave.

In hidden years, God is our only consistent audience. Others come and go, but only he always sees. God alone realizes our full potential and comprehends the longings in our souls. When no one else is interested in (let alone impressed by) our capabilities and dreams, God is still whole-heartedly with fatherly pride shouting his love over us.

Anonymous seasons afford us the opportunity to establish God as our souls' true point of reference if we resist underestimating how he treasures our hiddenness and take the time to decide whose attention and acceptance really matters in our lives.

PART FOUR

into the wilderness

CHAPTER

15 | the desert?

Then Jesus was led by the Spirit into the desert.
—Matthew 4:1

The sky ripped open, the Holy Spirit took the form of a dove and rested upon Jesus, God thundered his unfailing love from the heavens, and then he ushered his beloved Son into . . . the desert?

What? "I love you, Son. Enjoy . . . *the desert*"?

Generally speaking, this series of events makes us a little uncomfortable. Can following God's Spirit lead us straight into a desert? Would obedience deposit us in a wasteland? Could God's loving will direct us to wander about in barren places?

Evidently.

From Jesus' example, this appears to be true. We just do not talk about it often. Our earthbound hearts prefer to consider how following God leads us into happiness or health or wealth. "God led me into a desert! (hallelujah)" is just not the stuff T-shirts are made of.

Even so, did not Jesus' three decades of hiddenness already qualify as a desert experience? Yes. But in that desert of anonymity Jesus made peace with God's timing and concluded that Father God's companionship in his life was enough. From Jesus' perspective, his hidden years were good years: neither wasted nor unwanted. Therefore, we find no evidence of resistance when the Holy Spirit directs Jesus into another type of desert. Matthew simply states that Jesus was "led" there.

Desert is translated from a Greek word that refers to the abandonment of a person, cause, or place.[1] Though it can refer to a tract of arid, barren land or a waterless region, the primary meaning, when used to speak of a place, is that of *solitude* or *emptiness*. In this sense, *desert* is actually a descriptor for lonely places and uninhabited regions. Geographically, for Jesus, it probably referenced the untamed Judean wilderness east of the Jordan River. Lying between Jerusalem and the Dead Sea, this region featured dry wave upon dry wave of brown, barren hills where few things grew and fewer people passed.

Mark adds two more details to our image of Jesus in the desert: "He was with the wild animals, and angels attended him" (Mark 1:13). "Wild animals" sound slightly alarming, but the presence of angels is much more promising and was, no doubt, a source of great comfort to Jesus.

However, another presence was also in that desert whose agenda was anything but comfort—Satan. He seems to find his way into most deserts. Unpleasant, but anticipated, Satan's disagreeable company in the Judean wilderness appears to have been permitted by Father God himself.

In his love, God led his Son into a place that was a desert by every definition of the word: physically barren, emotionally lonely, and spiritually troubled. Though we have no record of God's voice speaking in the desert as it did at the baptism, we do know that Satan's voice was quite clear.

But the Judean desert for Jesus was not chapter 1 of his life —it was chapter 30. For almost three decades, Jesus had been making unseen choices throughout underestimated hidden years. During Jesus' anonymous season, his choices clustered and gained momentum. Now they would become the greatest influence on the decisions he faced during what was destined to become one of the most well-known experiences in all of history: the temptation of Christ.

CHAPTER

16 | to be tempted

Jesus' water baptism marked his first step out of hiddenness into documented, debated, scrutinized, and celebrated history. His second step took him from the cool waters of the Jordan into the dry wilderness of Judea "to be tempted by the devil" (Matthew 4:1).

The word *tempted* is translated from a verb that means "examine or test to learn another's true nature or character; try to trap or attempt to catch in a mistake."[1] When it appears as a noun, this same word is rendered as *temptation, testing,* or *trial* and is often used to describe the unglamorous realities of walking in faith.

> *Consider it pure joy, my brothers, whenever you face trials of many kinds, because you know that the testing of your faith develops perseverance. Perseverance must finish its work so that you may be mature and complete, not lacking anything.* ❧ (James 1:2–4, emphasis mine)

> *Dear friends, do not be surprised at the painful trial you are suffering, as though something strange were happening to you. But rejoice that you participate in the sufferings of Christ, so that you may be overjoyed when his glory is revealed.* ❧ (1 Peter 4:12–13, emphasis mine)

Both James and Peter call us to rejoice when we, like Jesus, experience testing times. They instruct us to anticipate them, persevere through them, and rest assured that in them we somehow participate in Jesus' sufferings.

In the midst of trials, however, we can find these encouragements easy on the eyes and hard on our hearts because trials are, by definition, trying! They reduce us, and in that reduction we wrestle fiercely with what we truly value and what we truly believe. That process can be exhausting emotionally, physically, and spiritually.

When pressed by testing, tempting times, it can strengthen our resolve to remember that trials and temptations are not the real enemy. Eternally, perhaps our greatest enemy on earth is losing perspective and beginning to value our fragile surroundings more than God's faithful friendship in our lives. From that point of view, if God's presence has led us into trying places, is there really any other place we would rather be?

For the love of his Father's close companionship, Jesus followed God's Spirit straight into the Judean wilderness. There, in the place of trial, Jesus had choices to make, just as we do.

> *Because he himself suffered when he was tempted,*
> *he is able to help those who are being tempted. . . .*
> *For we do not have a high priest who is unable*
> *to sympathize with our weaknesses, but we have*
> *one who has been tempted in every way, just as*
> *we are—yet was without sin.* ❧ (Hebrews 2:18;*
> 4:15)

Those who knew Jesus and/or were inspired by God's Spirit to write about Jesus asserted in unison that he was tempted, so I find it reasonable to conclude that Jesus was temptable. In the desert, Jesus was tried by Satan. His faith was tested. His soul was tempted.

In fact, according to the above passage from Hebrews, Jesus was tempted, "in every way, just as we are." Because he suffered through tempting, testing times, Jesus is able to wisely mentor us with sincere and great compassion through every trial and temptation we will face in this life.

That reality makes Jesus' example in the temptation more than worthy of our study and gives us cause to invest practical (not just theoretical) interest in the choices he made both before and during his wilderness experience.

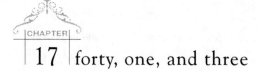

CHAPTER
17 | forty, one, and three

Forty days and forty nights . . .
—Matthew 4:2

Jesus was immersed in the refreshing waters of the Jordan for only a few seconds. His immersion in the temptation would last much, much longer. Obedience to Father God led Jesus to remain in the Judean desert more than forty days.

Fasting that length of time linked Jesus with the two greatest prophets of Jewish history: Moses and Elijah. This connection would have been extremely meaningful to the people of Jesus' day who were longing for God to send the Messiah.[1]

> *Moses was there with the LORD forty days and forty nights without eating bread or drinking water. And he wrote on the tablets the words of the covenant—the Ten Commandments.* ✽ (Exodus 34:28)

> *So he [Elijah] got up and ate and drank. Strengthened by that food, he traveled forty days and forty nights until he reached Horeb, the mountain of God. There he went into a cave and spent the night.* ✽ (1 Kings 19:8–9)

Much has been said rightfully and insightfully lauding the spiritual symbolism of the biblical phrase "forty days and forty nights." But having recently experienced a fortieth birthday (did I mention *very* recently?) I feel somewhat disinclined to join in the celebration. So, for the moment, let us just state the obvious and agree that forty days is a long time to be alone in a barren wasteland without food and harassed by Satan.

Think of these forty days as a window—the one I have been referring to throughout *anonymous*. Jesus' choices during the temptation open that window and grant us a view of his previous hidden years *because the choices we make in the place of trial today are greatly the fruit of choices we have made in our yesterdays.* Every documented choice Jesus made in the temptation reflects undocumented choices he was making *before* the temptation.

We actually started looking through this window and learning about the surprising power of hidden years at Jesus' water baptism—the first recorded moment of his adult life. There we saw that Jesus did not have to make a name for himself. His hidden years granted him (and can grant us) the space to make peace with God's pace.

We also witnessed Jesus' willingness to follow God wherever he led. Surrendering to hidden years enabled Jesus (and can enable us) to desire, above all, God's company and not be distracted by life's scenery. Over long, uncelebrated years while Jesus stewarded God-size dreams in anonymity, Father God had become his soul's true point of reference. That compass would serve him well as he walked into dry, troubled times.

Now we will explore how hidden years prepared Jesus to overcome three critical areas of temptation. Both Matthew's

and Luke's accounts of Jesus' time in the Judean wilderness record three interactions between Satan (who starts them) and
Jesus (who ends them).[2] We will base our study on Matthew's
ordering of these encounters.

Physically, the first interaction took place near some stones
in the desert, the second at the tip of the temple, and the third
on a very high mountain. Spiritually, though, these exchanges
had nothing to do with the environment, religious landmarks,
or random rocks.

Innumerable lessons could be mined in this biblical account.
But to assist us in concentrating on our theme of hiddenness,
we will view Jesus' experience in the Judean wilderness as one
singular temptation with three layers: appetite, applause, and
authority.

Though the layers vary in focus, the methodology Satan
uses in his attempt to trap Jesus follows a clear pattern. In each
layer,

- he dangles a *lure* (by offering Jesus something attractive),
- he exploits a natural *longing* (by appealing to an innately
  human desire),
- he identifies the *means* (by suggesting how Jesus can get
  what he wants), and
- he sounds a tempting *invitation* (by mixing truth with his
  lies).

Jesus' strategy in resisting temptation also follows a pattern.
In response to Satan's snare,

- ❧ Jesus first *anchors* himself (by looking to God and his Word), and then
- ❧ he makes a definite *choice* (that renders each layer's invitation ineffective).

Satan's basic methods have not changed since Jesus' stay in the Judean wilderness or, for that matter, Adam and Eve's stay in the Garden of Eden. The same tempting invitations have sounded throughout the centuries and still loudly command attention in our day. New packaging, for sure, but each shiny, modernized package contains the same tried-and-tired tune. Thankfully, the power of Jesus' choices has also *not* changed. His decisions—and the process by which he made them—can guide us safely through every tempting trial.

Forty days, one temptation, three layers. These forty days open a window for us into Jesus' past and the choices he made in unseen places during underestimated hidden years. As we examine his journey through the Judean desert, we will continue to gain insight into what Father God grew in Jesus (and what he seeks to grow in us) in anonymous seasons of the soul.

18 reflections

Time is not really spent. *Instead, it is invested in a future we cannot see.*

Though we know intellectually that the clock keeps ticking, we often—for a variety of reasons—fail to connect the choices we make in each tick and consider how that connection shapes our future. We feel the moment strongly but struggle to link a tangible today with an intangible tomorrow.

I have tried to emphasize this principle by viewing Jesus' journey in the Judean wilderness as one temptation with three layers as opposed to three separate, disconnected temptations. In fact, I see each layer as not only connected but as consecutive and cumulative. Each new layer increases the weight that rests on its predecessors.

Think of the temptation as a house with three stories. Our home only has two, but it will suffice as an illustration. You have heard of a fixer-upper? Well, we purchased sort of a second cousin to a fixer-upper; I called it a gutter-outer. The house was a mess, but my jack-of-all-trades (and master of most!) husband said it had a good, solid foundation for us to build upon.

Oooo-K, I thought as I looked around at the "I-am-about-to-be-sick" shade of yellow on the walls, the cracked and buckling five-layered linoleum, and the scruffy carpet that smelled remarkably like a petting zoo.

A few years later, Barry started drawing up plans to add a second story to our humble abode. During the process, he spent a lot of time in our poorly lit, dirt-floored, don't-even-think-about-standing-up crawl space. Since we were going to build up, I was puzzled that he was spending so much time under.

"I'm checking the support beams," he explained. "Going up adds weight and stresses the foundational beams. If they aren't strong enough, the added weight of new construction will cause the whole structure to collapse."

"Ah," I said reflectively and—being a writer, not a builder—I immediately thought of how the crawl space reminded me of hidden years. No one ever asks for a tour, but everything in our home is dependent upon what is under our home. The crawl space houses and guards our home's unglamorous guts. There we find the sturdy support beams, the heating and cooling ductwork, the main power line, and the water heater and filter and piping. It is all there, down under, hidden, but thankfully whole and in good order. Because the unseen has been carefully attended to, the visible can expand on a trustworthy foundation.

In the same way, people generally do not stand in line for a tour of our hidden years, which can be rather disheartening if we are in the habit of determining the value of our life's seasons by ticket sales. Though unpopular, these hidden places are not unproductive; within them God houses the unglamorous guts of a truly fruitful existence.

There in the poorly lit crawl spaces of life (transitions, prolonged waiting, new additions to the family, preparatory education, relocation, retirement, unexplainable loss, extended illness, irresolvable conflict, and all else that tends to hide us) God builds within us a sturdy support system for our souls. If we do not respect his craftsmanship in unapplauded seasons, all that is visible in our lives will rest on a fragile foundation, and eventually—through the added weight the visible brings—we will experience collapse.

Jesus' hidden years established a trustworthy foundation in his life. He resisted rushing and took the time to live them well. Now in the Judean wilderness each layer of temptation would rest on its predecessor (like a second floor does on a first floor) and double or triple the full weight bearing down on Jesus' hidden foundation. If there were any cracks in that foundation, the compounded stress of appetite, applause, and authority would reveal and exploit them. And if that hidden foundation was sound, all the temptations on the planet could not crush him.

Which returns us to a respect for time. Every choice we make is an investment in a future we cannot see. Some invest wisely. Some invest poorly. As the clock keeps ticking, the stresses of appetite, applause, and authority expose the state of our hearts and the stability of our souls. May the God of grace strengthen us to invest each tick well.

PART FIVE

the temptation
of appetite

CHAPTER

19 | the first lure

As we journey with Jesus through each layer of the wilderness temptation, we will first examine the substance of his encounter with Satan and then view that layer as a window opening backward in time into Jesus' previous hidden years.

We have little information regarding what transpired before day forty-one of Jesus' stay in the desert, but we do know that Jesus was not eating and we can guess that Satan was not sleeping. Their first recorded interaction begins with one of the great understatements of the Bible:

> *After fasting forty days and forty nights, he was*
> *hungry.* ✧ (Matthew 4:2)

Obviously God's Spirit supernaturally sustained Jesus during this period, or Matthew would have had to use another word as a substitute for *hungry*, like *starving, emaciated, unconscious,* or *hospitalized.* In his day, the word Matthew did select literally meant "to need food" and figuratively implied "to avidly desire something (as necessary to life)" which is why I refer to this portion of the temptation as the layer of appetite.[1]

In Jesus' state of hunger,

> The tempter came to him and said, "If you are the Son of God, tell these stones to become bread." Jesus answered, "It is written: 'Man does not live on bread alone, but on every word that comes from the mouth of God.'" ≫ (Matthew 4:3–4)

Webster defines *lure* as, "something that leads an individual into a place or situation from which escape is difficult."[2] Lures are tempting, attractive baits used to trap someone or something. Think of Satan's lures as truly tasty treats offered on camouflaged, razor-sharp hooks. The treats were real enough, but frankly, Satan was disinterested. He did not care any more about Jesus having a piece of bread than he did about Eve having a piece of fruit. For that matter, he still does not care whether we crave food or money or sex or control. His focus is the hook, and whatever fleeting pleasure we experience is worth it from his perspective as long as in the end he gets that hook into us.

In this first layer of temptation, Jesus was hungry, and Satan basically said, "What are you waiting for? Do something about it! Satisfy your need now." What Jesus was waiting for, though, was a release from the fast in particular and the Judean desert in general by Father God.

I find it noteworthy that Satan did not suggest that Jesus run into town and steal some food—that would have been a blatant violation of God's commandments. But eating? Food in itself is not sinful. And here is where Satan's lures can be deceptive. This layer was not about *what* Jesus would eat as much as it was about *when* Jesus would eat. Would he obey Father God even when obedience required delayed satisfaction of legitimate needs?

In the layer of appetite, we witness Satan's skillful use of a most effective lure: immediate gratification. Feel familiar? Surely this is still one of humanity's greatest weaknesses. In our day, we are unapologetically addicted to the immediate; we feel justifiably discontent with delay. Why should we wait when it is in our power not to?

Which is exactly the question Satan posed before Jesus: "Why continue in hunger when it is within your power to feed yourself?"

CHAPTER
20 | the first longing, means, and invitation

Effective lures exploit otherwise neutral human longings such as our natural yearning for sustenance, shelter, safety, relationship, pleasure, and significance. The first layer's lure of immediate gratification appeals to human appetite.

Like us, Jesus felt hunger and desired nourishment. His body required food. Though temptation in the layer of appetite often appeals to our *wants* and *passions*, in this instance Satan addressed an actual physical *need* in Jesus' life.

Then Satan identified, in a manner so concise that it was compelling, *the means* for how Jesus could obtain the lure and satisfy his natural longing. In layer one, he simply stated, "Tell these stones to become bread." How obvious was that? After all, this would not be the first time God provided bread for his people in the wilderness.

Almost fifteen centuries earlier, God freed his people from oppression in Egypt and with unfathomable patience led them on a journey through the desert. Though no longer in bondage to Egyptian masters, the Israelites were still slaves to their appetites:

> *"If only we had died by the* Lord's *hand in Egypt!*
> *There we sat around pots of meat and ate all the*
> *food we wanted, but you have brought us out into*
> *this desert to starve this entire assembly to death."*

> Then the LORD said to Moses, "I will rain down
> bread from heaven for you." ❧ (Exodus 16:3–4)

Obviously, the loud growls in the Israelites' stomachs were cre-ating service disruptions in their memory banks. But then, ra-tionalization reigns and history is revised when appetite rules. Perhaps Satan hoped that Jesus would stop at God's gracious provision in his recollection of this story. If so, he hoped in vain, as we soon shall see.

From the Greek texts, *"if you are the Son of God"* could also be translated *"since you are the Son of God,"* which may drasti-cally affect our understanding of what Satan was tempting Jesus to do. Consider how *if*—from the Greek particle *ei*—is used by Matthew elsewhere in his writings to capture dialogue (emphasis in these quotations is mine):

> If *that is how God clothes the grass of the field,
> which is here today and tomorrow is thrown into
> the fire, will he not much more clothe you . . . ?* ❧
> (Matthew 6:30)

> If *the head of the house has been called Beelzebub,
> how much more the members of his household!* ❧
> (Matthew 10:25)

> [Jesus] said to them, *"How is it then that David,
> speaking by the Spirit, calls him 'Lord'? . . . If then
> David calls him 'Lord,' how can he be his son?"* ❧
> (Matthew 22:43, 45)

Though *if* can be used to reference a questionable condition, depending on how it appears in combination with other words, it is also used (as demonstrated above) as a synonym for *because* or *since*. If the latter meaning is taken, then Satan was not saying, "If you are the Son of God, prove it!" but rather, "Since you are the Son of God, act like it!" What adds additional weight to this interpretation is the simple fact that there was no one in that desert who doubted Jesus' divine Sonship: not the angels who attended him, the wild animals who were created by him, or Satan, who showed up in person to tempt him. So whom would Jesus be proving himself to? In this layer of appetite, I believe that in his invitation Satan was tempting Jesus, not to prove himself, but to use his divinity to satisfy the needs of his humanity and avoid unnecessary pain.

In isolation, this suggestion may have seemed reasonable enough for someone who had been without food for forty days in a wilderness. But Jesus did not allow the moments of his life to exist in isolation. He constantly connected them and placed them in the light of God's will. Jesus knew that sacrificing his body on the cross in the future would be impossible if at this layer he chose to feed his flesh in the desert.

21 | the first anchor

Concentrating our attention on the tasty treat dangled before us is most unwise when we are tempted in the layer of appetite. This is the fatal mistake Eve made. She did not throw out an anchor to stabilize herself. Instead, Eve tried to navigate the temptation with her desires and passions at the helm.

When we commit this error in judgment, we fall prey to the *lie of just one*. We disconnect the moment of temptation from all other moments and dismiss our inner hesitations as overreactions because, we rationalize, this is only about *one* moment of splurging or *one* brief glance or *one* white lie or *one* . . .

Stifling any concerns of bigger-picture consequences, we take a bite. The sweetness that passes our lips quickly turns rancid as we begin to taste the cold, metallic hook in our hearts. Pleasure can anesthetize us against that taste temporarily, but when it wears off (which is inevitable) the pain or shame we feel serves to reconnect us with reality.

Jesus did not succumb to either dangle-dazzle or the lie of just one. Nor did the Son of God trust his emotions to navigate him through Satan's temptings. In the place of temptation, Jesus threw out a hook of his own—an *anchor* that caught firmly in something immovable—the Word of God:

> Jesus answered, "It is written: 'Man does not live on bread alone, but on every word that comes from the mouth of God.'" ⚬ (Matthew 4:4)

In this response, Jesus is quoting from the farewell address Moses gave around 1406 BC, two months before the Israelites finally entered their Promised Land. The passage is well worth referencing for our context:

> *Remember how the* L<small>ORD</small> *your God led you all the way in the desert these forty years, to humble you and to test you in order to know what was in your heart, whether or not you would keep his commands. He humbled you, causing you to hunger and then feeding you with manna, which neither you nor your fathers had known, to teach you that man does not live on bread alone but on every word that comes from the mouth of the* L<small>ORD</small>. *Your clothes did not wear out and your feet did not swell during these forty years. Know then in your heart that as a man disciplines his son, so the* L<small>ORD</small> *your God disciplines you.* ✺ (Deuteronomy 8:2–5)

How immediately applicable! Why does Father God lead those he loves into deserts?

- ✺ To humble us,
- ✺ to test us,
- ✺ to know what is in our hearts,
- ✺ to see if we will keep his commands,
- ✺ to teach us to depend upon him, and
- ✺ to discipline us as his children.

Jesus only cites one line of this passage from Deuteronomy, but in doing so he empowers his will with the whole story. In the desert, the Israelites had to completely rely upon God to supply food day by day. Provision would literally fall from heaven, but God *did not* permit the people to produce food for themselves. They were entirely dependent on him, and that helplessness tested them. Being powerless revealed what was in their hearts: would they, or would they not, obey God? From Father God's perspective, utter dependence, not self-reliance, is the true friend of our souls.

If anyone ever had the ability to completely live a self-reliant life, it was Jesus. But he passed on self-reliance. He knew it was highly overrated. As Jesus meditated on God's Word, that Word anchored and strengthened him to choose a better way in the desert.

22 | the first choice

What is our definition of *living*? When does it begin? How does it
actually end? What sustains it? What makes it precious? Could it
ever become worthless?

For Jesus, living meant much, much more than having food,
clothing, and shelter. He said, "Man does not live on bread alone,
but on every word that comes from the mouth of God" (Matthew
4:4). Did he need food? Of course. But there was something
he needed even more in order to truly *live*. How we define that
small word makes a big difference when we are tempted in the
layer of appetite.

In our sensory-driven world, it is easy to reduce our working
definition of *living* to the stuff we can touch, taste, feel, hear, and
see. Easy, but unwise. Such a reduction renders us vulnerable to
a deadly form of hopelessness when we experience pain-filled
trials or pleasure-less times. Additionally, it leaves us entirely de-
fenseless in temptations of appetite.

Jesus did not accept this definition. He believed that living
was initiated and sustained by God and therefore could not be
measured by the physical senses alone. *Life is* because *God is*.
We literally exist by the power of God's Word, and if he were to
withdraw that Word, all life would utterly perish.

This spiritual reality broadens our human responsibility sig-
nificantly past the gratification of our own senses to encompass
the honoring of God's Word that gives us life. As Jesus exempli-

fies, God's Word is not merely our anchor in temptation; it is the anchor of our existence.

In the Judean wilderness, that anchor proved faithful and enabled Jesus to resist Satan's lure through a world-changing choice. Though painfully conscious of his appetite, Jesus was even more purposefully committed to God's Word's having pre-eminence in his life. When tempted in the layer of appetite, Jesus chose to reposition his cravings, desires, longings, and physical needs behind God's unchanging truth.

Imagine how strongly Jesus' body must have protested this decision. Physically he longed for nourishment. Intellectually he knew there was nothing innately sinful about food. But his loyalty to his spirit surpassed his loyalty to his flesh. And in his spirit, he knew that using his power to satisfy his own appetite would be contrary to the will of Father God.

Before we, like Jesus, can position our roaring desires *behind* truth, we first have to distinguish our roaring desires *from* truth, and that is no minor task. Most of us have been quite success-fully conditioned to determine truth through the filter of our feelings: Do we feel it? Then it is true. Or so we are told.

But emotions are *not* truth's vocal twin, and feelings are not the litmus test for reality. Our emotions and feelings are sim-ply reactions to our environment, circumstances, and percep-tions. By nature they are followers, and we place our souls in danger when we require them to take the lead. Truth, on the other hand, was born to lead. God's truth clears the fog in our minds, provides much-needed boundaries for our emotions, and empowers our wills to choose well.

When tempted in the layer of appetite, it may sincerely feel as though we will die if our cravings are not satisfied. Actually, something does die when we reposition our feelings behind God's truth and refuse to let appetite rule: our*selves*.

23 | reflections

Though occasionally mistaken for one, I am not an optimist. I am a diplomatic realist, and it is easy to confuse the two. As a realist, I so appreciate that Jesus' chosen strategy to resist temptation in the layer of appetite was not denial. At best, denial seems a questionable use of our finite emotional resources. At worst, it is an intentional investment in untruth. Always, it is a poor defense against the lure of immediate gratification.

In the Judean wilderness, we do not find Jesus pacing about with determination chanting, "I am not hungry. I am not hungry. I am not hungry." He was hungry and made no effort to deny the existence of that hunger. When tempted by Satan to use his power to satisfy his own needs, Jesus' response was not, "What do you mean? I have no needs," but, "There is something I need even more than bread: my life is sustained by God's Word."

Victory over temptation was not on hold, waiting for Jesus' feeling of hunger to vaporize in the desert heat. Instead, victory was waiting for Jesus to reposition his felt appetite behind God's eternal will. That is not mere wordplay. It is a trustworthy strategy for not succumbing to temptation in the layer of appetite.

Easier said than done? Absolutely. In calling appetite a "natural human longing," I am not implying that natural is a synonym for passive. *Our appetites and their accompanying emotions are severely strong willed and do not gingerly volunteer to take the backseat in our lives. They prefer to drive, and we see the disastrous results of lives driven by appetite all around us.*

Countless forces resist this repositioning of our appetites and emotions. Consider a simple visit to a store. Advertisers are paid crazy sums to design emotionally compelling sales ads. With those sales ads in our hands and our minds determined to save money, we walk into a store that has been strategically laid out with impulse buying in mind. If, by divine intervention, we truly only buy what is essential, we are greeted at the checkout line with an invitation to take out a credit card, receive 20 percent off today's purchase, and delay our first payment for two years . . .

In some ways, our global economy thrives on enabling our appetites' addiction to immediate gratification. In such an environment, appetite has become the spoiled child of our culture: she gets what she wants when she wants it; otherwise she cries loudly. The emotional volume of that cry can be deafening, but it is either her tears today or our souls' tears tomorrow.

Ironically, even though repositioning our desires at first seems restraining, over time it is enhancing. Remember, feelings were designed to follow, not to lead. So when God's will and Word take the driver's seat in our lives, our feelings and desires are free to follow cleanly without regrets within safe boundaries.

When tempted in the layer of appetite, Jesus did not deny the existence of his natural longings and feelings. He did, however, intentionally upgrade the authority of his will by empowering it with God's Word. Personally, I like feelings— especially when they cooperate with truth. When they do not, though it is unpleasant, it is livable. They are followers, not leaders. And they can drag their sensitive little feet behind God's will and Word all the way to heaven!

PART SIX

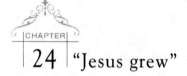

the fruit of
hidden years

CHAPTER

24 | "Jesus grew"

If Jesus' recorded, visible years open a window for us into his unrecorded, hidden years, what can we learn about the Father's work in the unseen, uncelebrated seasons of life?

Earlier we saw how, when faced with temptation in the layer of appetite, Jesus repositioned his feelings behind God's will and Word. In the desert, Jesus confidently responded to Satan's invitation with, "It is written . . . ," followed by a brief recitation from the book of Deuteronomy. At the risk of stating the obvious, it is very difficult to reposition our feelings behind God's will and Word if we are unfamiliar with God's will and Word. One simply cannot quote what one does not know. How then did Jesus become so intimately familiar with God's Word?

Could it be that Jesus (as both fully God and fully man) was graced with instant knowledge of all Scripture as fruit of his divine nature? In his writings, John does refer to Jesus as "the Word":

> In the beginning was the Word, and the Word was
> with God, and the Word was God. He was with
> God in the beginning. Through him all things were
> made. . . .
>
> The Word became flesh and made his dwelling
> among us. We have seen his glory, the glory of the
> One and Only, who came from the Father, full of
> grace and truth. ❧ (John 1:1–3, 14)

Here again, we are faced with the supreme mystery of the Incarnation. Yes, Jesus is *the Word*, but that Word *became flesh*. In becoming man, Jesus obviously accepted the temporary suspension
of divine attributes such as omnipresence. We also see that in
taking the form of man, Jesus accepted normal human development. In other words, physically Jesus was not born as an adult
but as a baby. He matured through all the awkward stages just
like any other boy. In fact, we read in Luke's writings that "Jesus
grew in wisdom and stature, and in favor with God and men"
(Luke 2:52).

Jesus *grew*.

During his hidden years, Jesus grew physically (in stature).
He grew relationally (in favor with man). We see as well that
throughout his anonymous season Jesus was growing spiritually
(in wisdom and in favor with God). He was not instantly all-
knowing. In fact, one of the rare snapshots we have of Jesus'
hidden years captures him asking questions:

They found him in the temple courts, sitting among
the teachers, listening to them and asking them
questions. Everyone who heard him was amazed
at his understanding and his answers. ✴ (Luke
2:46–47)

In *becoming flesh*, it appears that Jesus accepted the suspension
of divine omniscience. Year after year, he grew intellectually and
spiritually. Which returns us to our initial question: how then
did Jesus become so intimately familiar with God's Word?

25 | the preexisting word

Before Jesus declared, "It is written," we do not see him pausing to search for a concordance or looking about for his leather-bound pocket book of promises. Such things did not exist in his day. Most copies of the Torah (the Holy Scriptures) were in the honored possession of synagogues. These treasures were handwritten in Hebrew by highly skilled craftsmen on parchments made from the skins of ceremonially clean animals and then rolled onto ornately designed rods.[1]

The scrolls were so precious that readers used pointers, instead of their fingers, to follow the text and ensure that they neither dirtied the parchment nor missed a word. Perhaps the extremely wealthy could afford personal copies of the Torah, but from what little we know of Jesus' childhood, it seems unlikely that his home was graced with a sacred scroll.

So we can dismiss any images of young Jesus poring over the Torah at bedtime by means of an oil lamp. Jesus did, however, probably enjoy the privilege, as did most young men in his culture, of studying the Torah at a school attached to his local synagogue. But since Jesus could not carry home a copy of the Scriptures in his hands (for easy reference in times of need), he had to carry a copy of the Scriptures in his heart. In order for God's Word to have become that firmly embedded in Jesus, we are left to conclude that he must have spent considerable time meditating on and memorizing the Scriptures from what he heard or had the opportunity to read, which sounds like *work*.

What grows in anonymous seasons? The anchor of God's Word in our souls.

Hidden years provided the space for Jesus (and provide the space for us) to invest in Scripture meditation and memorization. Before we sigh in disappointment over our past failures in this area, it would be encouraging to note that Jesus quoted one sentence, not one hundred pages, from the Scriptures as he resisted temptation. God's Word is really quite potent! Meditating on and memorizing Scripture is not a feat reserved for those graced with photographic memories. Consistency, not speed, is the key to this adventure. What grows through the slow and steady practice of meditation and memorization is a truth anchor that holds even in the fiercest of storms.

I am eternally grateful to live in a day where the Bible is accessible in numerous forms for both literate and preliterate peoples. Our home happily houses dozens of Bibles in assorted shapes, sizes, and color combinations. But perhaps somewhere amid the overflowing accessibility of the Bible, we have somehow lost our awe of God's Word.

We rightfully revere the Bible. But before anyone ever put pen to papyrus or berry juice to a cave wall, God's Word *was*. God's Word is not a mere book. Our physical Bibles contain God's Word, but God's Word can never be contained by paper. The Word was in existence well before the inventions of the printing press, papyrus, or even stone tablets. I believe that Jesus took such care to meditate meaningfully on the Scriptures because he, more than anyone, knew that God's Word sustained all life.

Esteeming God's Word as even more than a treasured Bible

but as the initiator and preserver of our very lives will grant us the motivation necessary to reposition our resistant feelings behind God's preexistent truth. Disciplining our emotions and appetites is strenuous. But refusing (or simply ignoring) the life-sustaining, preexisting power of God's Word is spiritual self-sabotage.

CHAPTER

26 | the underrated virtue

Anonymous began with a reference to the iceberg equation:
10% visible + 90% unseen = an indestructible life

Icebergs do not grow their virtually indestructible strength top
down, but bottom up. Over countless millennia, falling snow
melts and refreezes layer upon layer, creating enormous ice
sheets over land and extending ice shelves over the sea. When
chunks break off these icy masses they are referred to as *icebergs*
and are monitored closely because of their profound effect upon
sea life and shipping.

The point being that an iceberg's strength does not emerge
overnight but grows slowly, layer upon layer, over time. Likewise,
Jesus' spiritual resolve did not suddenly materialize the moment
he stepped into the desert. His ability to throw out an anchor in
God's Word and reposition his roaring feelings behind God's will
was not an instant acquisition. That strength had been growing steadily in unapplauded places as Jesus developed a severely
underrated virtue.

What grows in anonymous seasons? Self-control.

Self-control is "the restraint exercised over one's own impulses,
emotions, or desires."[1] In other words, it is the ability to discipline our appetites.

The writers of the Bible speak highly of this quality. Peter identifies self-control as one of the essential building blocks of an effective and productive faith:

> *Make every effort to add to your faith goodness; and to goodness, knowledge; and to knowledge, self-control; and to self-control, perseverance; and to perseverance, godliness; and to godliness, brotherly kindness; and to brotherly kindness, love. For if you possess these qualities in increasing measure, they will keep you from being ineffective and unproductive in your knowledge of our Lord Jesus Christ. But if anyone does not have them, he is nearsighted and blind, and has forgotten that he has been cleansed from his past sins.* ❧ (2 Peter 1:5–9)

Paul refers to self-control in association with the work of God's Spirit within us:

> *The fruit of the Spirit is love, joy, peace, patience, kindness, goodness, faithfulness, gentleness and self-control. Against such things there is no law. Those who belong to Christ Jesus have crucified the sinful nature with its passions and desires.* ❧ (Galatians 5:22–24)

Both these passages emphasize that the development of self-control is part of an ongoing *process*. Peter speaks of possessing self-control "in increasing measure," and Paul refers to self-control not as a *gift* of the Holy Spirit but notably as a "fruit" of the Spirit. Like love and peace, self-control is not conferred or awarded; it is cultivated and accumulated.

Additionally, in his letters to Timothy and Titus, Paul lists self-control as a nonnegotiable quality of anyone placed in governing or mentoring roles[2] and as a virtue the learning generation should seek.[3] Which once again returns us to a respect for the hidden years.

People of all ages experience hiddenness. In fact, the poor navigation of hidden years later in life has ended more than a few souls' previously sweet legacy in bitterness. The challenges we face throughout the span of our lives certainly change, but our need for nurturing the discipline of self-control never expires.

However, perhaps no other space in life is more critical for the development of self-control than the hidden years of our teens, twenties, and thirties. In these early anonymous seasons, God graciously grants us the opportunity to wrestle with our appetites *before* other lives are at stake, to struggle with our passions privately before moral collapse affects the innocent publicly.

There, in the unphotographed spaces of hidden years, when we are not *calling the shots* or *taking the heat* or *on the frontlines* or *in the spotlight*, self-control has the opportunity to grow, slowly and steadily, layer upon layer, until all that inner strength fuses together and creates something indestructible.

CHAPTER

27 | a portrait of God

Temptation twists truth. When we hesitate (which we all too
often do) before a lure of immediate gratification, our minds can
feel overtaken by a sleepy fog called *confusion*. The longer we
stare at that lure, and the longer we wait to reposition our appetite behind God's will and Word, the fuzzier truth becomes in
our brains. Then we begin to question what we formerly thought
we knew: *Did God ever really say anything about this issue? Even if
he did, is it still relevant today? Besides, how can something that feels
this good be that bad? Certainly God wants us to enjoy the life he has
given us.*

Jesus halted this downward spiral immediately by looking
away from the lure and toward God's Word. Previously, we
examined how that choice was possible because of the self-
control and honor for God's Word Jesus developed during
hidden years. Another fought-for treasure that entirely influences our ability to resist temptation is also housed by hidden
years.

What grows in anonymous seasons? An accurate portrait of
God.

Anchoring ourselves in God's Word is close to impossible if,
in our hearts, we are unsure that God and his Word are *good*.
The waiting implicit in hidden years can compel us to wrestle
with the character—and at times, even the existence—of God.

When our dreams are delayed and our potential seemingly forgotten, we may question whether or not God loves us. When loved ones die and near ones leave, we may question whether or not we like God. These are the "if, then" queries of raw life:

If God is good, then why does evil thrive?
If God is all-powerful, then why does he not heal?
If God is all-knowing, then why does he not act?
If God is everywhere, then why aren't things different?
If God is real, then why can't I sense him?
If God is near, then why do I feel so forgotten?

Thankfully, God has survived such scrutiny before. He is, after all, a rather sturdy Fellow. Though he rarely answers our inquiries audibly, the important thing is that he stands beside us faithfully while we ask, while we wait, and while we weep.

Imagine the questions that Jesus might have had during his hidden years about the goodness of God and his timing. How must it have felt—knowing he had the power to heal—to have to walk past children suffering with leprosy? What would have run through his mind when—though he knew he was God's chosen Savior—he had to listen in silence as others doubted that the Messiah would ever come? What would it have been like—knowing that his conception was miraculous—to be unable to defend his mother when others whispered about her past? How hard would it have been—with unsurpassed wisdom growing in his soul—to sit passively while others taught what they did not live? And how agonizing would it be—when his Word could one day raise the dead to life again—to stand by while those he loved (perhaps even Joseph, his father) died?

"Why not now?!" is a cry that brings to the forefront what we actually believe about God. His timing, especially during hidden years, can offend our sense of justice:

> "My thoughts are not your thoughts,
>   neither are your ways my ways,"
>   declares the LORD.
> "As the heavens are higher than the earth,
>   so are my ways higher than your ways
>   and my thoughts than your thoughts." ⁊
> (Isaiah 55:8–9)

When our ways are not God's ways—though it may be unspeakably uncomfortable—we must wrestle with the discrepancy between what we think God should do and what he actually does and allow that struggle to edit our tidy, but tame, image of God.

If we wrestle with these questions with the lamp of God's Word by our side, an increasingly accurate portrait of God will emerge from our faith struggle, a portrait that is strong enough to trust in, good enough to wait for, and wild enough to never be contained in a box.

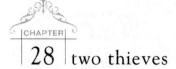

28 | two thieves

The Judean wilderness was surely not the first time Jesus experienced temptation in the layer of appetite. As a child obeying his parents, an adolescent doing his chores, a teen learning a trade, and a twenty-something watching his friends being paired off to start families, Jesus had plenty of opportunities to make choices and reposition his desires and longings behind Father God's will and Word.

During these hidden years, Jesus evidently did not underestimate the lifetime consequences of seemingly small, unseen choices in the realm of appetite. Otherwise, the temptation story would probably read quite differently.

In the daily rhythm of anonymous seasons, it can become exceedingly difficult to remember that every choice we make today influences a tomorrow we cannot see. When faced with temptation in the layer of appetite, two rationalizations in particular can rob us of the riches of hidden years by short-circuiting our long-term perspective.

The first thieving rationalization says, *It is just until . . .*

Returning to our banquet illustration from several chapters back, in hidden years we have a tendency to assume that *main* is somewhere out there, not right here. So we treat today with less respect than we should, as though the current gift of time before us is simply a filler.

In such an atmosphere, it is easy for us to rationalize indulging our appetites because, *Today does not really count*, or, *We will deal with the issue later*, or, *It will not make a difference now anyway*. All of which are blatant untruths. Today always counts. If we fail to deal with issues today, they will deal with us tomorrow. And choosing truth not only always makes a difference, it makes a difference that compounds exponentially to bless our future!

Living in the lie of *It is just until* . . . is like carelessly charging up a credit card because we are convinced that all charges will disappear at some future magical moment called marriage or employment or responsibility. Unwise indeed. Such choices can be forgiven. But the history created by such choices cannot be erased.

The second thieving rationalization that causes us to underestimate temptation in the area of appetite during our hidden years says, *It is better than* . . .

In this lie, we abdicate our responsibility to discipline our appetite by convincing ourselves that what we are doing is the "lesser of two evils." So we listen in silence to a slanderous rumor, but at least we did not start it. We punish someone repeatedly in our thoughts, but at least we are not doing it with our fists. We fantasize about impurity privately, but at least we are not engaging in it physically.

This kind of reasoning almost makes it seem as though we are doing God a favor by sinning, as though he should be satisfied or even proud that we are not doing something worse. But when tempted in the layer of appetite, the question we need to ask ourselves is not, *What is this better than?* but, *What is this feeding?* Whatever we feed will live to tempt us another day.

Consider the words of Paul:

> *Do not be deceived: God cannot be mocked. A man reaps what he sows. The one who sows to please his sinful nature, from that nature will reap destruction; the one who sows to please the Spirit, from the Spirit will reap eternal life.* ❧ (Galatians 6:7–8)

Two thieving rationalizations with one shared crime: when we say yes to temptations of appetite, regardless of our reasoning, we are choosing to feed sin that Jesus died for. That reality should break our hearts. It certainly has already broken his.

29 | reflections

Unlike Jesus, most of us do not deal in one sitting with all layers of temptation simultaneously. (Thank God.) Though the layers often overlap, our first spiritual challenges normally involve issues of appetite: our passions, emotions, cravings, and longings. I find that this layer stays with us throughout life much like a first floor in a house: it does not go away but is always in need of attention and maintenance.

Soon after, we may wrestle with applause: our desire for approval, acceptance, attention, and acclaim. For most, the temptation of authority comes with position, title, and responsibility and is a challenge reserved for our mid to later years.

We have all winced with pain over the sad stories of individuals who excelled early in life (perhaps in athletics or acting or some form of art) and as a result experienced all these layers at once. Few survive the premature, combined weight of money that can buy anything, admirers who will do anything, and the high-gloss brand of authority that comes with fame.

On the other hand, we have also been shocked by the seemingly sudden moral collapse of greatly respected and visible leaders in their golden years of influence. A new layer of authority added just the extra weight needed to reveal negligence in layers further down.

So we find heads of state confessing to destructive sexual addictions, CEOs cheating on their taxes, published professors erupting in explosive fits of rage, and world-renowned doctors coping with stress through dependence on prescription drugs. These dear souls can lead and even inspire others. They just cannot control themselves.

Appetite, it seems, is our most basic layer of vulnerability. No amount of education or height of accomplishment can substitute for self-control in the layer of appetite. Hidden years grant us the space to learn to discipline our passions, cravings, and desires. If we carelessly disregard this opportunity, sooner or later our negligence will undermine all else we have worked to achieve.

At heart, my husband and I are mentors. Regardless of what happens to be on our business cards, we are always investing in the next generation. Looking into their eyes, I know that the future is in the best of hands. But in love, I hope that their time to lead does not come to them even a moment sooner than absolutely necessary.

Over the decades, I have witnessed with tears the collapse of truly exceptional men and women who were crushed by the premature, combined weight of too much applause, too much authority, and too little self-control. So when I see those I mentor rushing toward the future or longing to be noticed or hungry for responsibility, I breathe a silent prayer: Oh, Jesus, grant them the gift of hiddenness. For a few more years, please let them grow in quiet anonymity.

Perhaps it is one of the most life-giving prayers I pray.

PART SEVEN

the temptation of applause

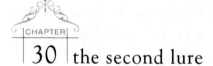

CHAPTER

30 | the second lure

Still searching for an unguarded weakness in Jesus to exploit, Satan switched bait in layer two of the temptation. Jesus had refused to perform a miracle to meet his own needs, but perhaps he would be willing to stage a miracle to meet the expectations of others:

> *Then the devil took him to the holy city and had him stand on the highest point of the temple. "If you are the Son of God," he said, "throw yourself down. For it is written: 'He will command his angels concerning you, and they will lift you up in their hands, so that you will not strike your foot against a stone.'" Jesus answered him, "It is also written: 'Do not put the Lord your God to the test.'"* ❧ (Matthew 4:5–7)

The scenery changed drastically as Satan took Jesus out of the empty, untraveled wilderness and into the populous, fought-for city of Jerusalem. There, away from the lonely desert and atop the lauded temple, Jesus again heard Satan's voice.

No doubt there were other famous cities that boasted tall buildings, but Jerusalem and the temple represented the very heart and hope of the Jewish faith. Jesus' first visit to this sacred place occurred when he was only eight days old. Thereafter, his family journeyed to Jerusalem annually for the Feast of the Passover.[1] As a child, Jesus referred to the temple as his "Father's house," and as a man, he would weep over the city of Jerusalem.[2]

Satan took Jesus to a city that had seen him committed to God through circumcision as an infant and would see him sentenced to death by crucifixion as an adult. Satan took Jesus to the temple, in the shadow of which Jesus had been praised as the Messiah by a prophetess and would be accused of blaspheming God by a priest.[3]

For Jesus, the spiritual significance of the temple in Jerusalem was weighty beyond words. Personally, it was a spiritual home for him. Socially, it was the focal point of his culture's faith representing the presence and protection of God. Politically, it was a potent religious symbol carefully monitored by the watchful eye of the Roman government that oppressed his people. Physically, it was where the people looked for him, as God's promised Messiah, to cast off Roman rule and establish his reign. Imagine all the thoughts that must have raced through Jesus' mind as he stood that day on top of the temple.

Below, the crowds were visible, but the worshipers probably were not individually distinguishable. Matthew records that Jesus stood at the *highest point*, or *pinnacle*, of the temple. The Greek word Matthew used means "a little wing" and probably refers to a wing-like structure of the temple roof. Traditionally, this location has been associated with the southeastern corner of the temple roof, which stood some 350 feet above the Kidron Valley below.[4] Another possibility is that the *pinnacle* referenced the southwestern corner, which is called the "place of trumpeting." The shofar was blown on this corner to draw the people's attention to important announcements or to usher in the Sabbath.

From either corner at that height, leaping off the roof would be suicide. But leaping off the roof and being rescued by angels would be spectacular. Standing on the temple's tip, Satan dangled before Jesus another enticing lure: mankind's attention and awe. He whispered, "Imagine what you could accomplish if you were viewed and pursued as spectacular."

31 | the second longing

CHAPTER

After thirty years of living in anonymity, attention alone would be tempting enough for most of us. But for Jesus, mankind's awe could have actually been useful because the people Jesus had come to save were expecting God's Messiah to make a rather grand entrance. Consider the following observations from *Matthew Henry's Commentary*:

> How subtle the Devil was, in the choice of the place for his temptations. Intending to solicit Christ to an ostentation of his own power, and a vain-glorious presumption upon God's providence, he fixes him on a public place in Jerusalem, a populous city, and *the joy of the whole earth*; in the temple, one of the wonders of the world, continually gazed upon with admiration by some one or other. There he might make himself remarkable, and be taken notice of by every body, and prove himself the Son of God; not, as he was urged in the former temptation, in the obscurities of a wilderness, but before multitudes, upon the most eminent stage of action.[1]

Because Jesus was the promised Messiah, this layer of temptation was infinitely more complex for him than it ever could be for us. But the lure Satan dangled before Jesus is still unspeakably attractive to our human hearts, because we all possess a natural longing for acceptance and applause. To be *accepted* is to be approved of, to be wanted, to belong. By *applause* I am not referring to an occasional "well done" but to the public affirmation of our value, giftings, and contributions.

A dear friend of mine, Sarah Herman, observed that one of man's fundamental desires is "to be celebrated." How true. There is something about being celebrated that satisfies a deep hunger in our souls. This longing for affirmation is not intrinsically evil. Our desire for acceptance predates the fall of man.

Humanity has never known existence outside of the context of relationship. In the beginning we were designed by God to desire acceptance and affirmation ultimately from him and also from each other. The longing for human affirmation in itself is not sinful. But living for that longing is both self-serving and shortsighted.

The satisfaction man's approval actually brings is always temporary. I liken mankind's acceptance and applause to rain: we appreciate it when it comes and yearn for it when it is gone, but we have precious little control over its coming or going. Human favor is both fickle and fleeting.

Jesus never lived for this longing. But as a man, his heart would certainly have been warmed by acceptance and affirmation and even applause. However, in the realm of longings, Jesus was able to distinguish between what was natural and what was truly needful. Man's affirmation was the former. God's affirmation was the latter.

CHAPTER 32 the second means and invitation

Standing on the tip of the temple, Jesus heard Satan's voice again:

> *"If you are the Son of God," he said, "throw yourself down. For it is written: 'He will command his angels concerning you, and they will lift you up in their hands, so that you will not strike your foot against a stone.'"* (Matthew 4:6)

Evidently, someone else had also been memorizing Scripture, which simply cautions us not to confuse reading the Bible with obeying God's Word. "Jump," Satan said. "God's Word promises to protect you."

Satan quoted from a section of Psalm 91 that begins in verse 9 with, "If you make the Most High your dwelling," and ends in verse 13 with, "you will tread upon the lion and the cobra." Not surprisingly, Satan opted to leave out these related verses and instead emphasized God's promise of protection without its preceding conditions or its intended outcome.

Perhaps Satan should have selected a different portion of Scripture, because the premise of Psalm 91 is that God protects us when we hide ourselves in him, not when we attempt to leap off buildings in a single bound:

> He who dwells in the shelter of the Most High
> > will rest in the shadow of the Almighty.
> I will say of the LORD, "He is my refuge and my fortress,
> > my God, in whom I trust."
> Surely he will save you from the fowler's snare
> > and from the deadly pestilence.
> He will cover you with his feathers,
> > and under his wings you will find refuge;
> > his faithfulness will be your shield and rampart.
> ❧ (Psalm 91:1–4)

Covered with his feathers. Under his wings. Behind his shield. Resting in his shadow. Surely these are some of the most beautiful images in Scripture of being peacefully hidden in God. Ironically, staying hidden was the antithesis of what Satan was tempting Jesus to do. Instead, Satan was inviting Jesus to use privilege and performance to win the approval of man. In other words, Satan was tempting Jesus to become a spectacle—for a good cause, of course: *stage something superhuman to draw people's attention to yourself and your message.*

Satan's temptations often muddy our noble intentions with his ignoble methods. For Jesus, man's attention and awe could have served a valid purpose. Would a miraculous introduction from the temple have hastened the people's acceptance of him as Messiah? *Probably.* Could widespread public admiration have created an environment more receptive to Jesus' radical teachings? *Most likely.*

So, would temporarily aligning himself with the people's expectations (of what the Messiah would be and how the Messiah would act) have facilitated the fulfillment of Jesus' ultimate mission more effectively? In a word, *no*. Spiritually, ends do not justify means. In fact, means seem to—for better or for worse— inevitably and irrevocably alter ends. More specifically, self-promoting means and methods have a way of mutating beyond recognition even the most selfless of original intentions.

33 | the second anchor and choice

Standing on great heights may make a few feel dizzy, but being tempted by great heights of people's acceptance and awe can cause any of us to lose our balance. Jesus, however, did not compromise his spiritual equilibrium for even a moment. He was anchored firmly in God's Word.

> Jesus answered him, "It is also written: 'Do not put
> the Lord your God to the test.'" ꙮ (Matthew 4:7)

As in the first layer of temptation, Jesus quotes one sentence in the book of Deuteronomy and in doing so strengthens himself with the whole story: "Do not test the LORD your God as you did at Massah" (Deuteronomy 6:16).

These words were spoken by Moses to the Israelites toward the end of their desert experience as they were about to enter the Promised Land. Though Massah may not be immediately meaningful to us, its mention most likely caused the Israelites more than a little discomfort.

Around three months after God had worked signs and wonders of deliverance in Egypt, the Israelites camped at a waterless place called Rephidim somewhere in the desert north or northwest of Mount Sinai. There we read that

> they quarreled with Moses and said, "Give us water
> to drink." Moses replied, "Why do you quarrel with

> *me? Why do you put the L*ORD *to the test?" But the
> people were thirsty for water there, and they
> grumbled against Moses. They said, "Why did you
> bring us up out of Egypt to make us and our chil-
> dren and livestock die of thirst?" . . . He called the
> place Massah and Meribah because the Israelites
> quarreled and because they tested the L*ORD *say-
> ing, "Is the L*ORD *among us or not?" ❧ (Exodus
> 17:2–3, 7)*

In other words, "Prove yourself, God. If you are really there,
then show us a useful sign." How often has God heard this taunt
across the centuries?

God's patience with our unappreciative attitudes of spiritual
entitlement is positively baffling, especially when we, like the
Israelites, have already been the beneficiaries of his abounding
grace and generosity. Consider all that the Israelites had witnessed to date in Egypt and even in their desert wanderings. At
Marah, they had seen bitter waters become sweet. In the Desert
of Sin, they had dined on quail and seen manna fall from heaven.
Their history, and our own experience, reveals that miraculous
signs do not automatically create within us either contentment
in our circumstances or confidence in God's future provision.

By citing this passage from Deuteronomy, Jesus links what Satan was inviting him to do on the temple with what the Israelites
had chosen to do at Massah. His urging Jesus to throw himself
off the temple with the expectation that God would send angels
to catch him was the equivalent of saying, "Is the Lord among us,

or not?" Jesus would have been forcing God's hand to prove his Sonship in spectacular fashion in the sight of all the people.

At Massah, the Israelites put God to the test by demanding that he prove himself through miraculous signs of provision. God's people tested him then, but God's Son would not test him now.

Jesus refused Satan's invitation by anchoring himself firmly in God's Word and choosing to honor God's ways and not live for man's awe. That anchor forged in his anonymous season held strong in the desert and throughout Jesus' public years, for this would not be the only time he was invited to use privilege and performance to win approval:

> *Then some of the Pharisees and teachers of the law said to him, "Teacher, we want to see a miraculous sign from you." He answered, "A wicked and adulterous generation asks for a miraculous sign!"* (Matthew 12:38–39)

> *Those who passed by hurled insults at him, shaking their heads and saying, "You who are going to destroy the temple and build it in three days, save yourself! Come down from the cross, if you are the Son of God!" In the same way the chief priests, the teachers of the law and the elders mocked him. "He saved others," they said, "but he can't save himself! He's the King of Israel! Let him come down now from the cross, and we will believe in him."* (Matthew 27:39–42)

From the tip of the temple, amidst the leaders and the crowds, and eventually upon a splintered, bloodied cross, Jesus saw clearly that honoring God's ways and living for man's awe were mutually incompatible life motivations. True then and still true today.

34 | reflections

When she was very little, my baby girl would do some extraordinary feat (like twirling around or jumping up and down) then turn toward us, pause with expectation, and finally say what she obviously thought we should have known: "You can clap now!" Which of course we all did with gusto.

My heart breaks when I see children who seem to have no one to clap for them. We all know that a child's future emotional well-being is greatly affected by the presence or absence of healthy, parental affirmation. When lacking, children can grow up to spend decades unconsciously searching for the "Well done!" they never heard from their dad or mom or caregiver. But even with parental affirmation (or several good counseling sessions), many of us still feel like children wandering about, waiting for someone, somewhere, to start clapping.

What do you wish others would clap about?

What could they affirm in you that would lead you to take a deep breath, sigh, and say, "Finally—I have been waiting to hear that for a long, long time"? Perhaps your . . .

    √ *contribution to the family ("What would we do without you?"),*

- accomplishments in the workplace ("You are the hardest worker I know."),
- inner character ("You are such an example of what we all should be."),
- material possessions ("You have the coolest stuff on the planet!"),
- money management ("I so admire your financial skills."),
- physical beauty ("You never seem to age!"),
- intelligence ("How I wish I had your brains."), or
- basic survival ("I am so amazed by how far you have come!").

Well, wait no more! Someone is clapping—wildly in fact. Father God never misses even a moment of our lives. His enthusiasm for us would make the most exuberant soccer mom look like a still-life painting.

The problem is that we can neither see him nor hear him. Thankfully, God's existence is not dependent upon a confirmation from our senses. His actions are not on pause awaiting our OK. Believe it or not, feel it or not, through Jesus, Father God accepts, affirms, and delights in his children.

Sometimes, though, this truth simply does not feel like it is enough, so we keep looking for "something more." That search has led more than a few followers of God to distraction, despair, or even self-destruction. Within our souls, we all possess an innate need to be soundly valued and wanted. Mankind's affirmation cannot probe the depths of that need

in our lives. Like a short spoon in a tall glass, people's attention simply cannot reach the bottom of our profound longing
to be valued. Only God can reach that place because he is the
One who created that place.

So when God's affirmation from above feels insufficient
and we are tempted to live for the awe and applause of man,
that is when we must combine the choice Jesus made in layer
two of the temptation with the choice he made in layer one.
We remind ourselves that honoring God's ways and living for
man's awe are mutually incompatible goals. Then we anchor
ourselves in God's Word and reposition our it-is-not-enough
feelings behind God's it-is-enough truth.

We are the recipients of God's enthusiastic attention and
acceptance. What could all the attention and acceptance of
the world actually add to that?

PART EIGHT

more fruit from hidden years

CHAPTER

35 | an unshakable identity

Jesus emerged from his anonymous season able to resist the all-too-enticing lure of man's attention and awe. We see this trait exemplified in the desert and throughout his public ministry. Praise slid off Jesus like water off a window. To have allowed it to collect would have warped the image of God others could see through his life. Even when pressured by adoring fans, Jesus was uninfluenced and able to continue with his plans:

> At daybreak Jesus went out to a solitary place. The people were looking for him and when they came to where he was, they tried to keep him from leaving them. But he said, "I must preach the good news of the kingdom of God to the other towns also, because that is why I was sent." And he kept on preaching in the synagogues of Judea. ❧ (Luke 4:42–44)

Jesus later would say, "I do not accept praise from men," and those who opposed him affirmed in frustration that this was all too true:

> *"Teacher," they said, "we know you are a man of integrity and that you teach the way of God in accordance with the truth. You aren't swayed by men, because you pay no attention to who they are."* ❧ (Matthew 22:16)

Jesus could not be manipulated. Why? What must have been growing in him during his previous thirty hidden years to grant him such immunity to the power of praise?

By definition, hidden years are uncelebrated years. These are the seasons when we feel underestimated, unappreciated, or even invisible. In other words, no one is clapping. In that silence, unsupported by rounds of applause, hidden years provide the opportunity for us to wrestle with what truly makes us significant. In the absence of others volunteering to explain why we are so valuable, we have to answer that question for ourselves.

This quest can be especially difficult when it is not anticipated, when we have known applause and perhaps even authority and find ourselves hidden *again*. Rarely does hiddenness visit us only once in our lifetimes.

The student who thrived in high school goes off to college and may suddenly feel like others see him as only a number. Years later, friends and family cheer at his college graduation, then he moves and realizes that once again he is relationally starting from scratch. Just as he is getting established at his job, he is transferred and finds himself in a new office where others do not know—and consequently are not impressed by—his past accomplishments. And many more seasons of hiddenness still await him: possibly marriage (with its own period of adjustment), perhaps parenthood (with its unsurpassed joys and unexpected costs), and hopefully retirement (with its theoretical gain of time and its factual loss of title).

In each season of hiddenness, our sense of value is disrupted. Stripped of what others affirmed in us, we are left staring at our undecorated selves, wondering what makes us truly special.

Surely no one experienced this disruption more drastically than Jesus. He came from heaven to earth, voluntarily stripped of his glory. Yet he does not seem to question the value of his undecorated self. During his hidden years, Jesus clearly came to terms with what made him significant. Actually, that *what* was a *Who*: the God whose love does not ebb and flow on the ever-vacillating waves of human perceptions.

What grows in anonymous seasons? An unshakable identity.

Through the first layer of the temptation we saw how hidden years provide the opportunity to develop an accurate portrait of God. In this second layer, we discover that hidden years also provide an environment in which we can develop a healthy portrait of ourselves.

Emerging from his anonymous season, Jesus had the strength to honor God's ways whether or not others were clapping for him. In unseen, underestimated spaces of life, Jesus developed an unshakable sense of identity that enabled him to not be manipulated by human affirmation and flattery.

The crowds could not control Jesus through the power of their emotions or the volume of their voices. This is especially significant in that Jesus' culture was not individualistic, it was communal. An individualistic culture might view not going along with the group as entrepreneurial. But in a communal culture, not being influenced by the group or being swayed by your family's opinions could have been viewed as disrespectful. Especially in his context, the immunity to people's praise that Jesus demonstrated (not only on the temple but throughout his earthly ministry) could only come from a strong sense of eternal significance.

That strength can be ours. It develops in seasons of anonymity as we fix our spiritual eyes on the God who can never forget our name.

36 | trust in God's timing

When tempted by Satan to use privilege and performance to win the approval of man, Jesus chose to honor God's ways and not live for man's awe. The unshakable identity we spoke of in the last chapter made the second half of that choice possible. But I believe another characteristic was also necessary in order for Jesus to make the first half of that choice.

What grows in anonymous seasons? Our trust in God's timing.

Hidden years are frequently marked by a loss of some control in our lives. This is certainly true when we enter hidden years involuntarily through illness, grief, relational crises, or tragedy. But it is also true when we enter hidden years willingly. (Just ask a new mom how in control of life she feels!) In anonymous seasons, it can seem as though we have lost control of our calendar; things generally do not happen according to our plans.

Much earlier in *anonymous*, we examined how Jesus must have awakened each day during his hidden years and asked, "Father God, are we there yet? Is today the day?" Day after day, month after month, year after year Jesus would have heard the same reply: "No, my Son. We are not there yet. Today is not the day."

Hearing those words can be excruciating when God-size dreams are bursting in our souls. Our potential feels all bottled up, as though it just might explode under the pressure, and we wonder, *When, my God? If not now, when?!*

During his visible years, Jesus would often be tempted by others to circumvent God's "when." Satan's voice may have been the first to suggest taking a shortcut, but it was neither the last nor the hardest to hear:

> *Jesus' brothers said to him, "You ought to leave here and go to Judea, so that your disciples may see the miracles you do. No one who wants to become a public figure acts in secret. Since you are doing these things, show yourself to the world." For even his own brothers did not believe in him. Therefore Jesus told them, "The right time for me has not yet come; for you any time is right."* ❧ (John 7:3–6)

Even Jesus' brothers questioned him about what on earth he was waiting for. What those closest to Jesus could not comprehend was that he was waiting for nothing on earth at all, not people's praise or an invitation from the leadership or even a window of opportunity. Jesus was waiting for God's revealed "right time."

That waiting placed his full potential on pause for decades. Yet we do not see him emerging from hiddenness with resentment in his heart. Nor do we find him, no longer hidden, rushing his acceptance as Messiah to make up for lost time. Over hidden years, Jesus decided that Father always knows best, that God's ways are perfect, and that he is never, ever late.

So when Satan tempted Jesus to jump-start his public ministry with a spectacular feat, Jesus was able to resist Satan and honor God's ways because he trusted in God's timing. On top of the temple, Father God was not saying *no* to Jesus' revealing himself as the Messiah but *not yet*. More than we can imagine rests on whether we will yield to God's *not yet*. The time would come when Jesus would defy death, not from a temple height, but from an empty tomb!

In hidden years, delayed dreams press the question of whom we will let hold the clock for the rest of our lives. When God's timing is not our timing and it is in our power to do something about it (as with Jesus' example on the temple), whose timing will we choose?

Ultimately, our answer to that question depends on whom we really trust.

37 | a disciplined imagination

In teachings that were recorded during his visible years, Jesus made it clear that God weighs our thoughts and actions equally:

> You have heard that it was said to the people long ago, "Do not murder, and anyone who murders will be subject to judgment." But I tell you that anyone who is angry with his brother will be subject to judgment. . . . You have heard that it was said, "Do not commit adultery." But I tell you that anyone who looks at a woman lustfully has already committed adultery with her in his heart. ❧ (Matthew 5:21–22, 27–28)

We are accountable before God for our imaginations as much as for our deeds. Since Jesus never sinned, we can safely conclude that he not only said *no* to living for man's awe *in his actions*, he also said *no* to living for man's awe *in his mind*.

On the tip of the temple, we know that Jesus did not take Satan's lure and jump physically. But it is important for us to realize that Jesus also did not take Satan's lure and jump mentally. By God's standards, if Jesus had said *no* to the former but *yes* to the latter, we would no longer call him "sinless." But Jesus did not stand there imagining how it would feel to be swept up by angels and surrounded by adoring fans. Even in his thought life, he refused to bask in the attention and awe of mankind.

What grows in anonymous seasons? A disciplined imagination.

Hidden years provide ample opportunity for us to discipline our minds. When we feel underestimated or unseen in real life, it is tempting to live out scenarios that make us feel wanted and recognized in our thought life. In seasons where we question our value, we can all too easily create—and frequently visit—an alternative version of life in our minds. Though such thoughts may provide temporary color to what we perceive to be an otherwise dull existence, they are still an investment in untruth.

This is not about the shutting down of our imaginations but the disciplining of them. There is nothing sinful about using our imaginations to become a polka-dotted dinosaur with a niece or to draw up plans for a dream home or to prepare for the vacation of a lifetime or to hope for a bright future with a loved one. What is under investigation here is our vain imaginations—those thought patterns that puff us up from the inside out or invite us to escape from reality and experience a more affirming existence in our minds.

Watching children exercise their imaginations to picture themselves as mommies, doctors, or astronauts is delightful; we call it playful *pretending*. As adults, though, there is a difference between using our imaginations to build a better tomorrow (being visionary) and mentally self-medicating through self-aggrandizing daydreams.

Disciplining our imaginations can be an enormous challenge, especially when we perceive ourselves as deprived of affirmation, attention, or acceptance. But in those seasons—perhaps even more so than in applauded seasons of influence—it is absolutely critical that we not live out in our thoughts what we know we should not live out in our lives. The principle we examined in layer one (when tempted by the immediate gratification of our appetites) is still true in layer two (when tempted in our thoughts by the attention and awe of mankind): we will reap what we sow, even in our minds (see Galatians 6:7–8).

For example, consider a new parent drowning in diapers who daydreams about the freedom and time he would have if he were still single or childless . . . who wakes up with less patience and more resentment toward his spouse and children. Or a woman lost in daydreams of being swept away by an attentive Prince Charming . . . who wakes up, rolls over, and wonders why her husband is looking more and more like a frog. Or a young professional smiling, lost in a daydream about high-profile companies fighting over him with ever-increasing pay scales and benefits . . . who wakes up somehow less satisfied and motivated in his current job.

Vain imaginations make us discontent with our current realities. The spiritual, moral, and relational repercussions of intentionally nurturing such discontentment can be devastating. Yet we often dismiss our daydreams as harmless, as though our minds were some sort of locked vaults where thoughts can live but never leave to infect the rest of our lives. Untrue. Our minds are not *contained* environments; they are *controlling* environments.

Would Jesus have been able to resist the lure of man's attention and awe on top of the temple if he had fed his imagination with daydreams of the crowds' attention and awe during his hidden years? No. May we likewise be careful in hidden years to not use our imaginations in a way today that will compromise our integrity tomorrow.

CHAPTER

38 reflections

I grew up with an addiction to fresh, whole milk. Between the two of us, my dad and I had a gallon-a-day habit. When Barry and I married, my parents sincerely considered buying us a dairy cow as a wedding present to help with our grocery expenses.

Then one day I turned thirty and quite suddenly felt uncomfortable. Going to the doctor and describing my symptoms, he asked coyly if I drank milk. Exercising my (rather developed) gift of suspicion, I said, "Maybe. Why?" He then explained his hunch that I had developed a lactose intolerance and suggested that I stop drinking milk for two weeks and see if the symptoms went away. Unfortunately, after trying his ridiculous suggestion, I felt much better, and over a period of, well, a long time, I finally weaned myself off whole milk and began drinking rice milk.

Pitiful. Really, rice milk should not even be allowed to have "milk" in its name. But I drank it because I knew it was much better for my body. Around two years later, my taste buds finally caught up with my brain, and today I am happy to say that I actually like rice milk, and at times even crave it (though I still think it should be renamed "rice juice" or "concentrated ricey beverage").

The point being that over decades I had developed a distinct taste for something that was no longer nutritious for me. For my health, I had to make a change. But even though that change was good for me, it took years before it tasted good to me.

That pattern mirrors my journey in this layer of temptation. Even with loving parental affirmation, as an atheist I was addicted to the attention and awe of mankind. I craved affirmation and longed to be spoken of in superlatives. Ultimately I was seeking a sense of lasting value, but it kept eluding me, like a rainbow always just over the next hill.

Then Jesus mercifully and dramatically interrupted my atheistic existence and within months began to expose the dangers of this addiction. Through his Word and his people, he revealed how vulnerable it made me to the power of others' praise, my own prideful perfectionism, and a whole host of other unpleasant spiritual ailments.

After spending decades developing a taste for mankind's attention and awe, I had finally realized it was not nutritious for my soul. Man's praise is like cotton candy—sugar-laden and insubstantial. For my spiritual health, I had to make a change. Though that change was good for me, it took years before it tasted good to me.

Once we have known an addiction to man's praise, shifting our diet from finding value in man's acceptance to finding value in God's acceptance does not happen in a matter of days. It is a process we revisit throughout our lifetimes. Thank God for hidden years! In those underestimated seasons, when no one shows up to decorate us with praise, life is finally bare enough for us to notice that God's adoring eyes have always been upon us. We had his attention all along. We just

*could not see it because we were too distracted by the sight of
ourselves.*

*Though I am far from completing that journey toward
an unshakable identity in God, and though I still struggle to
resist old habits, especially when disappointed or tired, I am
so grateful for how very, very sweet God's acceptance now
tastes in my soul. In him, the rainbow finally stood still. God's
enduring love has filled my soul with deeper satisfaction than
anything I have ever tasted in this world.*

*For those who know this struggle, I offer the following vul-
nerable prayer from the personal journal of Basilea Schlink:*

> Today I still long so much for honour,
> I am so pleased with myself, so rooted in
> my nature. I am pleased when others often
> ask for my opinion, when I am made to feel
> I am needed, when people know that I am
> clever, talented and popular. I am glad when
> I am friends with everyone, when I can
> share with others what is in my heart,
> when I can shine.
>
> But Lord Jesus, you were a servant of
> all. Today I surrender all desire to be great; I
> renounce all pleasure I take in being impor-
> tant. Help me never to take pleasure in the
> things that do not please you.[1]

PART NINE

the temptation
of authority

CHAPTER

39 | the third lure

Since Jesus' hunger for bread or applause paled in comparison
with his hunger to obey Father God, Satan continued his tempting with something much bigger and brighter:

> *Again, the devil took him to a very high mountain
> and showed him all the kingdoms of the world and
> their splendor. "All this I will give you," he said, "if
> you will bow down and worship me."* ❧ (Mat-
> thew 4:8–9)

> *The devil led him up to a high place and showed
> him in an instant all the kingdoms of the world.
> And he said to him, "I will give you all their au-
> thority and splendor, for it has been given to me,
> and I can give it to anyone I want to. So if you
> worship me, it will all be yours."* ❧ (Luke 4:5–7)

On an unnamed mountain peak, Satan made a business proposition to Jesus. The goods were weighty, but the exchange would be private. No one but Jesus and Satan would know the transaction's terms, at least no one on earth.

Satan was literally offering Jesus the world. Not the world to come (for that was not Satan's to give) but this present world, the inhabited earth, which—disturbingly enough—was his to give. In Jesus' own words, Satan is the "prince of this world."[1] Even after Jesus' resurrection, the apostle Paul still referred to Satan as "the god of this world."[2]

Though real, Satan's rights on earth are not unlimited; otherwise the planet would certainly be in a much greater state of crisis. Nor is Satan's reign eternal:

> The seventh angel sounded his trumpet, and there were loud voices in heaven, which said: "The kingdom of the world has become the kingdom of our Lord and of his Christ, and he will reign for ever and ever." And the twenty-four elders, who were seated on their thrones before God, fell on their faces and worshiped God, saying: "We give thanks to you, Lord God Almighty, the One who is and who was, because you have taken your great power and have begun to reign." ❧ (Revelation 11:15–17)

One day, at the sound of a trumpet, the final residue of Satan's reign on earth will be swept away forever. But during the temptation, while he stood with Jesus on the mountain, Satan's offer was valid. He was able and willing to sell what remained of his lease on planet earth.

In addition to the world's natural resources, Satan offered Jesus the world's political, human, and economic resources. *Kingdom* in the passage quoted earlier refers to the great realms, empires, nations, and territories of the earth. *Authority* captures both the power and the right to rule over others. *Splendor* describes not just beauty but breathtaking beauty. Matthew used this word later in his writings when he quoted Jesus as saying, "And why do you worry about clothes? See how the lilies of the field grow. They do not labor or spin. Yet I tell you that not even Solomon in all his *splendor* was dressed like one of these" (Matthew 6:28–29, emphasis mine) *Splendor* refers to all that radiates richly, glitters gloriously, and shines with magnificence.

In an instant, Satan showed Jesus all the riches of the world. Imagine the view! Jesus saw untamed oceans and snow-capped mountains, tropical forests and untouched deserts, exotic birds and wild beasts, and—most importantly—people. From that panoramic peak, the Son of God saw stretched out before him a treasure he would not see again until he returned to heaven: a great multitude from every nation, tribe, people, and language.[3] He saw the earth's true riches; the souls he came to die for.

In this third layer of the temptation, Satan dangled before Jesus a lure of earthly power and possession. All that astonishes, all that amazes, all that the world could possibly boast of . . . it could all belong to Jesus, for a price.

CHAPTER

40 | the third longing, means, and invitation

To be honest, at first glance I did not find Satan's lure in this layer of the temptation that enticing. Bread would be tempting if I were hungry. People's awe would be tempting if I were discouraged. But earthly power and possession? I struggle to keep my own house clean; what would I do with a whole planet? Then it became clear that Satan was not merely dangling before Jesus more stuff and bigger barns but the right to rule the world.

What would you do if you were the sole, supreme ruler of all nations and peoples on earth?

With that power you could . . .
- end child prostitution,
- make sure no one ever died of hunger again,
- find a home for every homeless soul,
- protect the helpless,
- provide jobs for the jobless,
- pursue justice for the oppressed,
- channel money toward truly worthy causes,
- ensure that the elderly were never abandoned,
- prosecute drug traffickers,
- create the best environment possible for those with special needs,
- offer a college education to every desiring student,
- make sure everyone had adequate medical care,

- ✣ create and enforce laws to detox the environment,
- ✣ protect our natural resources,
- ✣ remove abusive world leaders, and
- ✣ end most wars before they began.

Now *that* is enticing.

Earthly power and possession appeal to our innate desire for influence and authority. We all have a natural human longing to make a difference in this world. When corrupted, this longing only serves ourselves. When kept pure, this longing truly serves humanity.

Satan suggested to Jesus a means by which he could immediately fulfill that longing: "'All this I will give you,' he said, 'if you will bow down and worship me'" (Matthew 4:9). Satan's word choice paints an astonishing picture. *Bow down* refers to an intentional and voluntary posture of submission. *Worship* is a word reserved for showing homage to a superior, as the Magi did to Jesus:

> *After Jesus was born in Bethlehem in Judea, during the time of King Herod, Magi from the east came to Jerusalem and asked, "Where is the one who has been born king of the Jews? We saw his star in the east and have come to worship him."*
> *. . . When they saw the star, they were overjoyed. On coming to the house, they saw the child with his mother Mary, and they bowed down and worshiped him.* ✣ (Matthew 2:1–2, 10–11)

Not even angels allowed people to bow down and worship them. In the book of Revelation, the apostle John was so overwhelmed by everything he was seeing that twice he bowed down before an angel and tried to worship him:

> I, John, am the one who heard and saw these things. And when I had heard and seen them, I fell down to worship at the feet of the angel who had been showing them to me. But he said to me, "Do not do it! I am a fellow servant with you and with your brothers the prophets and of all who keep the words of this book. Worship God!" ✤ (Revelation 22:8–9)

Basically, the angel said, "Would you stop doing that! There is only One who's worthy of worship, and I am not *him!*"

Satan was not *him* either. Nonetheless, he wanted Jesus' worship; it was worth more than the world to Satan. In this layer, Satan invited Jesus to sell his soul to purchase the world. Jesus had come to suffer for sinners. Satan suggested that he sin to avoid suffering. Jesus had come to die for the world. Satan offered him the world without dying.

41 | the third anchor and choice

The world is pretty weighty, but Jesus' anchor in God's Word still held fast. As he did in each interaction with Satan, without debate or even discussion, Jesus quoted truth from the Scriptures:

> *Away from me, Satan! For it is written: "Worship the Lord your God, and serve him only." ✻ (Matthew 4:10)*

Here again, Jesus turns for strength to a passage from Deuteronomy:

> *Fear the LORD your God, serve him only and take your oaths in his name. Do not follow other gods, the gods of the peoples around you; for the LORD your God, who is among you, is a jealous God and his anger will burn against you, and he will destroy you from the face of the land. ✻ (Deuteronomy 6:13–15)*

These verses immediately precede the sentence we examined in layer two regarding Massah. They were part of the instructions Moses gave to the Israelites as they were about to leave the wilderness and enter the Promised Land. On the edge of the desert, physically and spiritually, Moses set this choice before the people: worship only God or pay for idolatry with your life.

Centuries later, Jesus stood on the edge of his wilderness experience, recalled Moses' admonition, and declared his choice to *worship and serve God alone*. From the top of that mountain, the vista was captivating. But nothing in heaven or earth was worth more to Jesus than Father God's presence.

So Satan could keep the world, and Jesus would keep his soul. A few short years later, Jesus would explain his reasoning to a flustered friend:

> *From that time on Jesus began to explain to his disciples that he must go to Jerusalem and suffer many things at the hands of the elders, chief priests and teachers of the law, and that he must be killed and on the third day be raised to life. Peter took him aside and began to rebuke him. "Never, Lord!" he said. "This shall never happen to you!" Jesus turned and said to Peter, "Get behind me, Satan! You are a stumbling block to me; you do not have in mind the things of God, but the things of men."* ❧ (Matthew 16:21–23)

Peter tried to convince Jesus to avoid the cross—once! Jesus' response probably shocked his dear friend. But in Peter's suggestion, Jesus smelled the lingering, foul scent of Satan's all-too-familiar temptation: *sell your soul to purchase the world*.

> *Then Jesus said to his disciples, . . . "Whoever wants to save his life will lose it, but whoever loses*

> *his life for me will find it. What good will it be for*
> *a man if he gains the whole world, yet forfeits his*
> *soul? Or what can a man give in exchange for his*
> *soul? For the Son of Man is going to come in his*
> *Father's glory with his angels, and then he will re-*
> *ward each person according to what he has done."*
> ❧ (Matthew 16:24–27)

Jesus' thoughts about gaining the world were not mere hypotheti-
cal musings. The world had been for sale before for the price of
a soul—his. But once you sell your most precious possession you
have nothing else left that can buy it back. In that sense, souls
are not sold; they are forfeited.

Satan's offer was real but shortsighted. He tempted Jesus to
give up his soul permanently to gain the world temporarily. He
offered Jesus his off-brand imitation of glory from the world and
forgot that Jesus already possessed the original from heaven. In
essence, Satan asked Jesus to trade the *eternal* for the *visible*,
which is something he still invites us to do every day.

In small, undocumented choices throughout hidden and public
years, Satan continues to offer us the world in exchange for our
souls. Occasionally he still uses mountaintops, but more often he
shows us the view from laptops, checkbooks, boardrooms, corner
offices; he takes us behind closed doors, onto trading floors, up
on stages, and in front of microphones.

Like a shrewd salesman, Satan customizes his offer for each
person. The view changes, but the price is fixed. Considering
what is at stake, it would be wise for us to know what views make

us most vulnerable. What could he show you that would tempt you to bow down and worship him? Power or pleasure? Old scars or new possessions? The past or the future? Where does he take you to entice you to forfeit your soul?

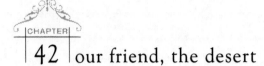

42 | our friend, the desert

Not immediate gratification, nor man's attention and awe, nor even the world's power and possessions—none of Satan's age-old lures had succeeded in capturing his prey. In the barren desert, on the temple's tip, and from a mountain height, Satan's strategies had all failed. In his planning, he had obviously underestimated what had been growing in Jesus during his hidden years.

The Tempter, however, was far from giving up. At Jesus' command, Satan left. But as Luke records, his leave was only temporary:

> *When the devil had finished all this tempting, he*
> *left him until an opportune time.* ❧ (Luke 4:13)

Opportune time refers not to spots on the clock but to strategic moments. Satan would return to tempt Jesus in the future at decisive points of vulnerability. Though Jesus knew he would see Satan's seductive lures and hear his smooth voice again, he was no doubt grateful for the Tempter's departure.

Thus ends Jesus' stay in the stark, empty desert. For more than forty days he had wandered through the barren brown hills of the Judean wilderness. After such a grueling physical and spiritual experience, it would be reasonable to assume that Jesus would never want to see a desert of any shape or size again for the rest of his life! Reasonable, but not accurate.

As mentioned previously, the word *desert* in the Scriptures is not necessarily a reference to oceans of dry sand but to any empty or abandoned place or thing. As Jesus stepped out of the Judean wilderness and into the public eye, he did not avoid such lonely spaces. On the contrary, he pursued them for the rest of his days. The same word that is translated *desert* in the temptation appears throughout Jesus' visible years as *solitary* or *lonely* places. (The emphasis in all the verses quoted below is mine.)

> *When Jesus heard what had happened, he withdrew by boat privately to a* solitary *place.* ❧ (Matthew 14:13)

> *Very early in the morning, while it was still dark, Jesus got up, left the house and went off to a* solitary *place, where he prayed.* ❧ (Mark 1:35)

> *Because so many people were coming and going that they did not even have a chance to eat, he said to them, "Come with me by yourselves to a quiet place and get some rest." So they went away by themselves in a boat to a* solitary *place.* ❧ (Mark 6:31–32)

> *At daybreak, Jesus went out to a* solitary *place.* ❧ (Luke 4:42)

> *Yet the news about him spread all the more, so that crowds of people came to hear him and to be*

> *healed of their sicknesses. But Jesus often withdrew*
> *to* lonely places *and prayed.* ❧ (Luke 5:15–16)

Jesus headed for the desert early in the mornings, in times of grief and times of joy, even in the busiest of seasons, and especially at the height of his popularity. He frequently withdrew to quiet, abandoned places where he could be alone with his Father God. These still, empty spaces were soothing for Jesus' soul. In practice, Jesus called the desert his friend.

Throughout Jesus' documented, celebrated years, people still saw only the tip of the iceberg of who he really was and what he had really come to do. So even when his life was no longer hidden, even when his days were painfully public, Jesus still cultivated a holy place of hiddenness within his soul.

During his uncelebrated anonymous season, a quiet reserve had been building within Jesus where he savored God's sweet fellowship undistracted by whatever circumstances happened to surround him. That sacred space is where God sees before man sees, where unfulfilled longings are stored even in visible years.

In the holy place of hiddenness, dreams and devotion thrive. That spiritual space is refreshed in lonely places; it is well watered by deserts. May that sacred space always be well watered in us. Then, when possessions and power do come, we will be quick to use them for God's glory and not for our own.

CHAPTER

43 | reflections

I still remember the sound of the dry, pebbled sand crunching beneath the car's wheels as it passed through the metal gates and into Canaan in the Desert. Exhausted, I had come to this refuge in Arizona for a prayer retreat that marked the beginning of my first sabbatical season. For nine days I walked throughout the beautiful desert garden with tears in my eyes, grieving over something I could not name.

More than ten years earlier, Jesus had mercifully interrupted my life. In gratitude I pursued him, his Word, his people, and his purposes with passion. But somewhere along the way I began giving out to others more than I was building up within myself. At the time, it did not make sense. I kept going through my mental checklist of everything I knew to do to mature in God: Devotional life? Check. Disciplined Bible study? Check. Worship? Check. Repentance? Check. Community? Check. Service? Check. The checklist seemed to be helping me help others grow, but I still could not escape the sense that something within me was dying.

Up until this time, I had focused primarily on Jesus' teachings and resurrection. In the desert I found my attention being drawn toward his sufferings and crucifixion. Sitting for hours before each station of the cross, I was taken by Jesus' humility in the face of indescribable pain. He could have

shown his power but instead assumed a posture of
holy weakness.

   This humble posture characterized Jesus' entire life:
his patience throughout unapplauded anonymous seasons,
his identification with sinners in the waters of baptism, his
willingness to be led into the desert temptation, and his ability
to deflect praise and embrace rejection in his visible years
of ministry.

   As Paul said in his letter to the Philippians, "Your
attitude should be the same as that of Christ Jesus: Who,
being in very nature God, did not consider equality with God
something to be grasped, but made himself nothing, taking the
very nature of a servant, being made in human likeness. And
being found in appearance as a man, he humbled himself
and became obedient to death—even death on a cross!"
(Philippians 2:5–8).

   Jesus' true strength was not revealed in his ability to
teach and lead the multitudes. It was manifested in his willingness to make himself nothing, to suffer, and to die. I had
enough strength to exhaust myself studying, mentoring, and
teaching, but I did not possess sufficient strength to be nothing.

   In the desert I slowly began to realize that such enduring
spiritual strength is the fruit, not of movement, but of rest; not
of activity, but of stillness. Whatever the context, Jesus could
stand strong in public because he stood still in private. He
intentionally pursued quiet places to be alone with his Father
God. Such is the opportunity deserts afford.

Many of us avoid lonely spaces because, by definition, deserts are barren. Nothing seems to grow there. But perhaps that is the point. Growth is so very distracting. Deserts are bare, but they are also beautiful. They are empty, but there is healing in their stillness. In those beautifully barren, empty, still spaces, our faith is uncluttered as we rest in God alone.

On my last day of that visit, I spent the morning at the foot of a tall wooden cross. It was rough, cracked, and wonderfully weathered. Many pilgrims had been there before as the dozens of rocks of remembrance displayed. Ten years earlier Jesus had saved me from my sins. Adding my small stone to the pile, I realized that Jesus was now offering to save me from myself.

I rose to leave that day with John the Baptist's words echoing in my soul: "He must become greater; I must become less" (John 3:30). John's longing is the seed of true spiritual strength. How surprising to discover that it grows best when planted and tended in deserts.

PART TEN

the crowning fruit from hidden years

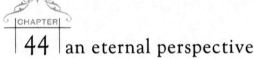

CHAPTER

44 | an eternal perspective

Jesus was able to walk away from the splendor and authority of all this world's kingdoms. How? What must have been developing in Jesus during long, hidden years to enable him to refuse the lure of earthly power and possessions?

On the surface, this third layer of the temptation presents a truly bizarre scenario: Satan (a fallen angel) was offering Jesus (the Creator incarnate) the world (which Jesus created and Satan now rules):

> I will give you all their authority and splendor, for
> it has been given to me, and I can give it to anyone
> I want to. So if you worship me, it will all be yours.
> ✲ (Luke 4:6–7)

Satan openly and accurately admitted that he is not the first owner of the world. The First Owner, obviously, was God. Satan also acknowledged that all his earthly authority was *given* to him.

You can only receive authority from someone who has more authority. Who was this Someone? Again, the answer is God. Additionally, Satan made his offer to Jesus, the Word, the Messiah, through whom all things were made, before whom angels fall down and worship. Who was Jesus? God's Son.

Satan stood on the mountain height before Jesus and in essence said, "I will give you what used to be yours, if you give me what has never been mine. All you have to do is trade places with me: you can become ruler of the world if I can become your god."

What was Satan hoping for in making this offer to Jesus? Earlier we examined all the good that could possibly be accomplished if someone were the sole, supreme ruler of the planet. Perhaps Satan hoped Jesus would seize the chance to make an immediate difference globally instead of beginning with a few souls locally. Or, since Jesus had already waited long decades in hiddenness, perhaps Satan hoped he had grown impatient and lost trust in God's timing. Or perhaps Satan hoped that Jesus' trying experience in the desert would convince him to avoid suffering in the future.

Personally, I think Satan's real hope was that Jesus would somehow—because of the heat or the hunger or the loneliness or the sheer dazzle of the world and its splendor—lose sight of eternity even for a moment and forget who he really was. Because it is when we forget who we are that we are most vulnerable to bowing down.

But Jesus did not lose sight of eternity. He remembered that he had been with Father God in the beginning and would return to Father God at the end of his earthly life. He remembered that in gaining the world momentarily, he would lose his soul eternally. And no doubt he remembered that though Satan might rule the earth for an age, the nations had been promised to him as his inheritance long, long ago:

> I will proclaim the decree of the LORD:
>> He said to me, "You are my Son;
>> today I have become your Father.
> Ask of me,
>> and I will make the nations your inheritance,
>> the ends of the earth your possession."
> ⤞ (Psalm 2:7–8)

What grows in anonymous seasons? An eternal perspective.

Like a presenter blinded by lights on a stage, we can often lose our perspective in the glare of the world's deadly glitter. Hidden years, however, remove us from the world's hot spotlights and restore our spiritual vision. No longer hypnotized by earthly power, possessions, or praise, we can once again distinguish between the temporal and the eternal. Consider these words from the apostle Paul:

> Though outwardly we are wasting away, yet inwardly we are being renewed day by day. For our light and momentary troubles are achieving for us an eternal glory that far outweighs them all. So we fix our eyes not on what is seen, but on what is

unseen. For what is seen is temporary, but what is
unseen is eternal. ❧ (2 Corinthians 4:16–18)

During his hidden years, Jesus developed eyes to see the eternal. That perspective guided him safely past every glittery and dazzling lure in this world.

45 | submission-based authority

Though many other qualities could be explored, the final treasure of hidden years that we will focus upon in *anonymous* will
probably be the most unexpected.

What grows in anonymous seasons? Submission-based authority.

Allow me to quote from an earlier chapter:

> "I want to walk like Jesus walked and live like
> Jesus lived!" is generally *not* equated in our
> hearts with, "I want to live 90 percent of my life
> in absolute obscurity!" No. Our desire to "be
> like Jesus" contains several exemption clauses,
> not the least of which are Jesus' hidden years,
> desert experiences, temptations, tortures, and
> crucifixion. We will pass on those, thank you.
> What we *are* most definitely interested in, how-
> ever, is Jesus' character and authority. How we
> long to see his character and authority trans-
> form this broken world through our lives!

Immediately, as Jesus emerged from the temptation, people were
captivated by the same attribute that captivates us today: his

amazing authority. Jesus' public years were marked by a continual stream of comments about his unusual, somewhat startling,
authority:

> *When Jesus had finished saying these things, the
> crowds were amazed at his teaching, because he
> taught as one who had authority, and not as their
> teachers of the law.* ✣ (Matthew 7:28–29)

> *The men were amazed and asked, "What kind of
> man is this? Even the winds and the waves obey
> him!"* ✣ (Matthew 8:27)

> *The people were amazed when they saw the mute
> speaking, the crippled made well, the lame walking
> and the blind seeing. And they praised the God of
> Israel.* ✣ (Matthew 15:31)

> *They went to Capernaum, and when the Sabbath
> came, Jesus went into the synagogue and began to
> teach. The people were amazed at his teaching, be-
> cause he taught them as one who had authority, not
> as the teachers of the law.* ✣ (Mark 1:21–22)

> *All spoke well of him and were amazed at the
> gracious words that came from his lips.* ✣ (Luke
> 4:22)

They were amazed at his teaching, because his message had authority. ❧ (Luke 4:32)

"No one ever spoke the way this man does," the guards declared. ❧ (John 7:46)

Jesus' authority surprised people. They felt it was different from anything they had ever witnessed before. Why?

The people often contrasted Jesus' authority with that of the Pharisees and the teachers of the Law. Though these leaders were probably less than blessed by the comparison, the fact is they had very real authority. They identified themselves as disciples of Moses and children of Abraham.[1] Jesus himself said that "the teachers of the law and the Pharisees sit in Moses' seat. So you must obey them and do everything they tell you" (Matthew 23:2–3). The authority of the religious leaders flowed from positions they occupied by ancestry or appointment in their religious community.

Satan also had very real authority on earth, which he tried to sell to Jesus for the price of Jesus' soul. He explained that he had the right to offer Jesus the world, "for it has been given to me, and I can give it to anyone I want to" (Luke 4:6). Such words imply that Satan's authority to barter the planet as the "prince of this world" flowed in part from possession: you own the stuff; you make the rules.

Certainly the people were familiar, as we are, with this possession-based form of authority. And they obviously were familiar, as we are, with position-based authority. Yet Jesus' authority was still a mystery to them because it was not derived

from worldly possessions: lay before him the treasure of the
Magi or strip from him his only tunic; his authority remained
unchanged. Nor was Jesus' authority derived from earthly positions: crown him King or dismiss him as a criminal; his authority
remained unchanged.

Jesus' authority flowed not from possessions or positions but
from *submission*. What was the surprising source of Jesus' authority? Submission to his Father's will and Word.

Throughout the temptation, Jesus reaffirmed with every
"It is written" the same decision he had been making quietly in
unapplauded places over uncelebrated years during his previous
thirty hidden chapters of life: *I will live in submission to my Father's
will and Word.*

Over the years, Jesus' consistent choice to submit to his Father God's will and Word clustered and built momentum as he
stepped out of his anonymous season and into the waters of the
Jordan River. There, the Holy Spirit descended not on talent,
title, or worldly possessions but upon the submitted heart, mind,
and spirit of Jesus.

That combination is authoritative! That combination influences history. That combination can be greatly served by possessions and positions but never completely contained by them.
That is the combination that awakens sleeping souls and alters
the destinies of peoples and nations: the amazing, awakening,
submission-based authority of Jesus.

Who could have imagined?! The attribute that seems completely absent in our hidden years is the very one that God is developing in us as we submit to him in unseen places, moment by
moment and year by year: authority! The authority that grows in

anonymous seasons is deep and enduring because it is not based on positions or possessions that appear one day and are gone the next but on submission to our eternal God.

"I want to be like Jesus," we say with sincerity. "I want to walk like Jesus walked." Then may our loving Father God help us begin submitting like Jesus submitted. That quest begins in anonymous seasons as we offer the prayer that guided Jesus through the darkest moments of his life: "Not my will, but yours be done."[2]

46 | a powerful duet

Jesus' submission-based authority was disturbing to the religious
and political leaders. His very presence was indisputably authoritative. For people who only knew the authority that flows from
positions or possessions, Jesus' authority would have been absolutely unnerving.

Consider the following interaction between Jesus and Pilate, the
Roman procurator of Judea (a political leader by appointment):

> *The Jews insisted, "We have a law, and according
> to that law he must die, because he claimed to be the
> Son of God." When Pilate heard this, he was even
> more afraid, and he went back inside the palace.
> "Where do you come from?" he asked Jesus, but
> Jesus gave him no answer. "Do you refuse to speak
> to me?" Pilate said. "Don't you realize I have power
> either to free you or to crucify you?" Jesus answered,
> "You would have no power over me if it were not
> given to you from above."* ✸ (John 19:7–11)

Imagine how Pilate must have felt standing before Jesus—
a man of no rank, no title, and no wealth—who possessed more
authority than Pilate had ever known. Or think of how the chief
priest, elders, and temple guards felt when they came to arrest
Jesus with clubs and swords and saw Jesus heal the severed ear of
one of their servants then turn to his own disciple and say,

> *"Put your sword back in its place, . . . for all who*
> *draw the sword will die by the sword. Do you think*
> *I cannot call on my Father, and he will at once put*
> *at my disposal more than twelve legions of angels?*
> *But how then would the Scriptures be fulfilled that*
> *say it must happen in this way?"* ❦ (Matthew
> 26:52–54)

Observing their servant's whole ear and Jesus' restrained disciples, they must have thought, *Yes. Thank you, I think. Can we go now, sir?* This is sort of like pretending to tame a wild elephant when the truth is he happens to be going in the same direction you are.

Submission-based authority equipped Jesus to be at peace standing before political rulers and spiritual leaders even when he was being falsely accused and wrongfully sentenced. Since others did not give him his authority, others could not take it away. Submission-based authority thrives with or without man's praise and approval.

Though Jesus' authority was unfamiliar to the people and their position-based religious and political leadership, it is important for us to remember that submission and position are not antonyms. They simply represent different dimensions of very real authority. Titles, credentials, and positions are not evil. On the contrary, they are essential.

We need position-based authority in this world. Can you imagine what chaos would ensue if there were no earthly positions of authority? We would rush to a hospital emergency room, ask to see the head physician, and be told, "Head *what?* We have no titles in this place. We are anti-credential because they create elitist hierarchies."

A society without titles and positions, with no special regard for degrees and credentials, where everyone is equally encouraged to do everything, may initially appear enlightened and egalitarian—until you need a brain surgeon! Then, all of a sudden those specialized degrees, temporary titles, earned credentials, and distinguishing positions start sounding very important.

Positions are vital in the world and equally so in the community of faith. Throughout the Scriptures we see God establishing positions of spiritual authority, such as those filled by the religious leaders of Jesus' day.

Position and submission are not mutually exclusive dimensions of authority. In fact, when they walk hand in hand they sing a powerful duet! When people who cultivate submission to God's will and Word in the holy place of hiddenness are placed in spiritual positions of authority, the results are world changing! Publicly, they stand before others and lead, but privately they continue to kneel before God and learn.

A world of good can be done, both in the world and in the church, when positions of authority are filled by people whose lives have authority. And a world of damage can be done, especially in the church, when individuals who have ceased to—or possibly never even started to—cultivate continual submission to God dare to assume positions of spiritual leadership in the community of faith:

position + submission = empowering leadership
position – submission = abusive leadership

47 | warning signs

Most of us will at some point in life emerge from hiddenness and encounter the temptation of authority in the world and/or in the community of faith. The challenges presented by this layer of temptation are unique, unlike anything we face in the layers of appetite or applause.

If we have taken the time in unseen, uncelebrated spaces to develop an eternal perspective and submission-based authority, we will find ourselves strengthened to resist corruption in the day of power and influence. If not—without the discipline of submission to God's will and Word—I believe it is virtually impossible for spiritual leaders, in particular, to not become abusive.

The cultivation of submission-based authority in the holy place of hiddenness was so essential to Jesus that he reserved his harshest rebuke for those who held titles of authority but whose lives had no authority. Since power can corrupt even the most gentle of hearts, and since Jesus obviously took this issue seriously, it is worth our time to examine the warning signs of souls that delight in position but no longer live in submission to God's will and Word.

In the day of title, position, and power, we should be very alarmed if we discover the following in our lives.

   ❧ We stop practicing what we preach:

> *The teachers of the law and the Pharisees sit in Moses' seat. So you must obey them and do everything they tell you. But do not do what they do, for*

they do not practice what they preach. ❧ (Matthew 23:2–3)

Holding a position of authority over others, yet not living in
submission to God in our hearts, breeds a dangerous lack of ac-
countability in our souls. Without the discipline of submitting
our plans, thoughts, and actions to God's will and Word, an un-
censored gap forms between what we require of others and what
we require of ourselves. Position then becomes an exemption
from obedience. We should be alarmed if we hear ourselves giving others good advice that we no longer personally heed.

❧ We begin specializing in the creation of rules:
    They tie up heavy loads and put them on men's
    shoulders, but they themselves are not willing to lift
    a finger to move them. ❧ (Matthew 23:4)

When position-based authority is not accompanied by
submission-based authority, the resulting spiritual leadership is
often characterized by the endless creation of rules and regulations. Generally, these lists of laws are rationalized and justified as
a means of helping others avoid sin. But I have often wondered
if the real motivation is avoiding failure (sinful or not), both individually and corporately. Leaving no room for error drains the
very life out of learning. When our goal shifts from *growing* to *not
failing*, something has become off-center in our lives.

❧ We stage displays of our devotion:

Everything they do is done for men to see. ❧
(Matthew 23:5)

Position is a dimension of authority given to us by other people. Without the peaceful confidence that submission-based authority provides, we can begin acting as though it is always an election year, continually campaigning for people's admiration. Much more than affirmation, the people's vote means job security for the position-based leader. When we find ourselves pausing so that someone else can see us, we need to ask ourselves what we are doing when no one is looking.

❧ We feel deserving of special honor:

They love the place of honor at banquets and the most important seats in the synagogues; they love to be greeted in the marketplaces and to have men call them 'Rabbi'. ❧ (Matthew 23:6–7)

Submission to God in the holy place of hiddenness reminds us regularly of God's acceptance and grace. Exposed continually to his love, we develop a healthy and sturdy sense of self-worth. Without that exposure, leaders can search for self-worth comparatively: being given the bigger office or the better view, being greeted by so many people that others have to wait for you, or seated not just *near* the head but *at* the head of the table.

When receiving honor is no longer humbling, we need to take note. A great deal of difference exists between feeling honored and feeling worthy of honor.

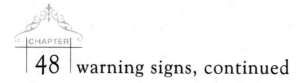

48 | warning signs, continued

Continuing our thoughts from the last chapter, in the day of title, position, and power we should be very alarmed if the following begin to occur:

❧ We lose sight of the sacred:

> *You also say, 'If anyone swears by the altar, it means nothing; but if anyone swears by the gift on it, he is bound by his oath.' You blind men! Which is greater: the gift, or the altar that makes the gift sacred?* ❧ (Matthew 23:18–19)

In order to submit to God, we must both love him and trust him. So when we cultivate a submissive spirit, we are also cultivating a worshipful spirit. In their religious detailing of levels of oath-taking, the position-based leaders Jesus was referring to had lost sight of true worship. When we, like them, become focused on regulations and formalities, we gut worship of its sacredness by reducing offerings to assets and altars to furniture.

❧ We tithe our money but are stingy with our mercy:

> *You give a tenth of your spices—mint, dill and cumin. But you have neglected the more important matters of the law—justice, mercy and faithfulness.* ❧ (Matthew 23:23)

Position-based leadership has a curious obsession with things that are countable. Excessive interest in that which can be quantified, measured, and objectively assessed reveals a lack of appreciation for the unseen, the immeasurable, and the eternal. Submission to God in the holy place of hiddenness gives us an appreciation for the latter. If we major on tithing but minor on mercy, major on attendance to church but minor on faithfulness to our families, we have probably lost the spirit of God's laws in our pursuit of the letter of God's laws (which I believe is the definition of legalism).

> ❧ We consciously conceal our hypocrisy:
> *You clean the outside of the cup and dish, but inside they are full of greed and self-indulgence. . . . You appear to people as righteous but on the inside you are full of hypocrisy and wickedness.* ❧ (Matthew 23:25, 28)

Here Jesus draws attention to leaders who feign righteousness but are indulging in intentional sin. This level of known, willful duplicity is only possible if we refuse to cultivate submission-based authority. To submit to God's will and Word is to submit to the conviction of God's Holy Spirit. If we as leaders profit from hypocrisy, we will answer dearly to God, who weighs the thoughts of every heart.

> ❧ We overestimate our immunity to sin:
> *You say, 'If we had lived in the days of our forefathers, we would not have taken part with them in*

shedding the blood of the prophets'. ❧ (Matthew
23:30)

Submission to God's will and Word brings us face to face with
his holiness and our humanity. In the light of God's purity, we
realize there are very few things we are incapable of doing. God's
Word is like a mirror in that it reveals to us our true nature. That
realistic portrait causes us to pause before we belittle others' weaknesses or consider ourselves immune to others' failures.

> ❧ We silence the voice of the prophet and wise man:
> *I am sending you prophets and wise men and
> teachers. Some of them you will kill and crucify;
> others you will flog in your synagogues and pursue
> from town to town.* ❧ (Matthew 23:34)

In their nervous protection of title and status, position-based
leaders have little tolerance for being corrected. They dare not
risk the possibility of being wrong. Prophets, wise men, and
teachers are therefore a threat, one that is often silenced quickly.
While submission-based authority maintains a teachable spirit,
position-based authority assumes it has no need for further in-
struction. Such leadership closes itself off from critique, even
when the messenger is sent from God.

Seeing ourselves in any of these signs should bring us to
our knees in prayer. Not in hopelessness, but in a sincere cry for
God's help. For some, that cry may lead us to step away from
our positions for a season and ensure that submission-based
authority is once again growing in our lives. For the sake of

our souls and the souls of those we lead, we cannot afford to hold spiritual positions of authority when our lives do not have the authority that is only derived from submission to God's will and Word.

Submission-based authority develops in us the strength of humility. Position-based authority makes us vulnerable to the dangers of hypocrisy. When position and submission walk together, the combination is spiritually life-giving. When position walks alone, the consequences are literally heartbreaking.

49 | reflections

Where are we in reference to the day of position and influence?

For some, that day is in the future. We are in school, in training, in transition, in diapers, in a holding pattern, or in a desert. Each morning we wake up and pray Jesus' hidden-years prayer: "Father, are we there yet? Is today the day?" And each morning we hear the same reply: "No, my child. We are not there yet. Today is not the day."

The encouraging news for the still-hidden is that the amazing, awakening authority of Jesus does not suddenly appear when we have our business cards printed. That dimension of authority grows steadily as we continually submit ourselves to God's will and Word in unseen and uncelebrated places. Submission-based authority does not need an invitation from either title or position to begin making a difference in a world of need.

For others, the day of position and influence is now. Today we are in charge, at large, in front, and in control. Today we are leading, managing, organizing, advising, teaching, directing, guiding, and going. Some are in the spring of this season, and the weight of influence feels uncomfortable and a little bulky. Some are in the summer of this season and feel the past prepared them for this very moment. Some are approaching the winter of this season and see a time in the near future when they will resign positions and others will assume their present roles.

The encouraging news for the no-longer-hidden is that
the amazing, awakening, startling authority of Jesus that we
cultivated in anonymous seasons carved out a strong inner
stream of humility in our souls. If we continue to nurture that
stream in quiet, lonely places, submission-based authority
will safeguard us in the seductive days of position and title
and strengthen us to use our influence for God's glory, not
our own.

And for others, it seems that the day of position and
influence is already behind them. Having passed their titles
on to the next generation, they have released their successors
to take new risks and repeat old errors. A few are relaxing,
grateful for a space in life that lacks the stress and pressure
of positional responsibilities. A few are busier than ever with
projects and travel and family. And a few feel a bit useless as
they stare restlessly into the future, wondering why it is called
"the golden years."

The encouraging news for the hidden-again is that the
amazing, awakening, startling authority of Jesus in us never
retires and never resigns. Titles and positions were its servant,
not its source.

A man of God who had served for decades in national
positions of spiritual leadership once described some of the
drastic changes that occurred when he resigned his title. Immediately, his speaking invitations diminished from a raging
river to a rarely flowing brook. Within a few short years, he
was no longer receiving honorary registrations to conferences
and complimentary tickets to yet another banquet. He was
no longer called upon to facilitate task forces or participate

in committees. Leaders stopped seeking his opinion; in fact, leaders stopped seeking him, as though he had never existed or contributed or served.

But as I mentioned, he was a man of God. Throughout the visible years of position and influence, he had not neglected the holy place of hiddenness. All along he had been sitting at the feet of Father God in loving submission to his will and Word. Later, after his title had been resigned, he still overflowed with the amazing, awakening, startling authority of Jesus. That unusual authority drew the spiritually hungry of a new generation to voluntarily sit at his feet and learn.

Thinking of him (and countless others who have served faithfully for decades and now feel justifiably forgotten) causes me to question whether we applaud in each other what Jesus applauds in us. Perhaps we give applause too easily, and perhaps we strip it away too quickly.

Positions come, and positions go. The recognition we know today can easily evaporate tomorrow. But that is OK. It is all right, because when we stand before Jesus the question he is going to ask us will not be, "Were you accurately estimated? Were you appropriately recognized? Were you sufficiently applauded?"

Those questions will not even come close to making the list when we see Jesus face to face. But other questions will make the list, and I desperately want to be prepared for them. I want to be prepared for the day he looks me in the eye and asks, "Did you love me? Did you love others toward me? Did you obey me? Did you submit yourself to my will and my Word? Did you live for what I died for?"

The pre-tests for that final exam are not held when I am signing a book or speaking on a stage. The pre-tests for that moment occur in uncelebrated places, in private thoughts, in unseen attitudes, in secret chambers of my heart—hidden to others but always visible to Father God. In the end, I long to see him look over these tests, smile and say, "Well done."

PART ELEVEN

guarding the holy place of hiddenness

CHAPTER

50 | only one

The camouflage is updated from generation to generation, and the bait is adjusted from person to person, but all of us are invited into the same age-old trap. Ultimately, that trap has little to do with bread or temples or kingdoms or this habit or that relationship or this pain or that memory.

For Jesus in the desert, and for us throughout our lifetimes, there is really only one true temptation in our spiritual lives: *to choose against God.* Satan's sole goal is to somehow invite us—and in some way entice us—to disobey, even in the smallest way. Our disobedience is his prize, because he knows something that we are often in denial about. He knows that disobedience cannot be confined to one concealed corner of our lives. Refusing quarantine, it spreads like a mold, continually stretching its infectious fingers toward previously uncontaminated spaces in our minds.

In his effort to entice humanity to rationalize choosing against their God, Satan has been skillfully throwing out his seductive lures since the Garden of Eden:

> ✤ immediate gratification to appeal to our appetites,
> ✤ man's attention and awe to appeal to our longings for acceptance and applause, and
> ✤ the world's power and possessions to appeal to our desires for influence and authority.

When we compare the lures he used to tempt Jesus in the wilderness with the "good for food and pleasing to the eye, and also desirable for gaining wisdom" fruit Satan tempted Eve with in the Garden, two facts become evident:[1]

1. Satan is predictable.
2. In thousands of years, we have not given him any reason not to be.

Generation after generation, we continue to crave instant satisfaction, daydream of public admiration, and be hypnotized by worldly power and possessions. Thankfully, in word and deed, in anonymous spaces and public places, Jesus modeled for us the most effective strategy against the tempting efforts of Satan: *unmodified obedience*.

> *I will not speak with you much longer, for the prince of this world is coming. He has no hold on me, but the world must learn that I love the Father and that I do exactly what my Father has commanded me.* ✤ (John 14:30–31)

Jesus did not add to or subtract from what Father God asked him to do. He did not embellish it, dilute it, tailor it, or customize it to suit his personal tastes or preferences. Jesus simply and profoundly obeyed. Unmodified obedience—not personality or opportunity or human favor—is the faithful guardian of God's will in our lives.

Such obedience safeguarded Jesus' spirit and divine calling as he journeyed unnoticed through thirty hidden years, as he wandered alone for forty days in the stark Judean desert, and as he made his three-year pilgrimage, surrounded by crowds, toward a rugged, merciless cross:

> *When the devil had finished all this tempting, he left him until an opportune time. Jesus returned to Galilee in the power of the Spirit, and news about him spread through the whole countryside. He taught in their synagogues, and everyone praised him.* ᔔ (Luke 4:13–15)

Jesus walked out of the temptation uncompromised and into the crowds with humble confidence. In Father God's loving wisdom, he had held back the showers of people's praise in his Son's life until chapter 30, after twenty-nine years of obedience-inspiring, character-carving drought. Reflecting on Jesus' long anonymous years and the unprecedented challenges of his documented visible years, we realize that God does not hide us to punish us, but to protect us.

As it was with his Son, so it is with us: being hidden by God's hand is a good and perfect gift.

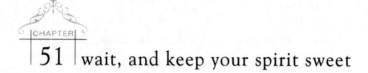

51 | wait, and keep your spirit sweet

Though unapplauded, our anonymous seasons are not even remotely unproductive. In them, God cultivates strengths that stand the test of time:

- the anchor of God's Word
- self-control
- an accurate portrait of God
- an unshakable identity
- trust in God's timing
- a disciplined imagination
- an eternal perspective
- submission-based authority

Such strengths are not *given*; they are *grown*. They are the fruit of active participation, not passive observation. Anonymous seasons can be the most spiritually fruitful spaces of our lives *if* we respect their potential and cooperate with God in their development.

How can we welcome our hidden years and fully realize their potential?

Wait because he is worthy.
Keep the waters of your spirit sweet.
Befriend stillness.

Wait because he is worthy. Tending sheep in anonymity, David was anointed king as a ruddy teenager by Samuel. Though the prophet brought the anointing oil, he left David's crown at home! David waited more than a dozen difficult years after his anointing before he actually became king at the age of thirty.[1]

Has it ever felt as though God poured his kingly dreams all over you but left the crown at home?! We are not the first to have God-given but unfulfilled dreams simmer in our souls during hidden years.

After God promised to make her husband into a great nation, Sarah waited twenty-five years before she held Isaac in her arms.[2] After God gave Joseph dreams of leading his family, he waited over twenty years before he even saw them again and was able to rescue them from famine.[3] After Moses' failed attempt to help his oppressed race, he waited forty years before hearing God's voice call him to lead his people out of slavery.[4] After becoming queen, Esther waited almost twenty-five years before her "such a time as this" moment came and she stood in the gap for her people.[5] After his stunning spiritual encounter, Paul waited more than ten years before he was officially commissioned by the church to the ministry for which we know him today.[6]

Forty, twenty-five, twenty, ten . . . not minutes or months but years! However, if we wait one year, let alone one decade, we begin to despair that God has forgotten us. Along with stillness, another discipline we must rediscover if we are to fully harvest our hidden years is *waiting*. Sometimes we sabotage our future by refusing to wait upon God in our present.

Spiritually, waiting is more than resigning ourselves to delayed dreams because we have no other option. Waiting is also more than the patient endurance of the passage of time. Waiting captures a prayerful posture in our spirits of purposeful attentiveness toward God: looking toward him, longing for him. We wait upon him, not for what we hope to receive, but because of who he is. God is worthy to be waited on, whether or not we hear anything, whether or not we see anything, whether or not our dreams are fulfilled.

We all have dreams hidden in our hearts. We protect them, prepare for them, and treasure them with anticipation. But what will become of them?

Personally, I do not know whether my God-given dreams will be fulfilled in this lifetime or whether my tears and prayers are watering them for a future generation. I do not know if, like Joshua, one day God will say, "Be strong and courageous," and march me straight into the realization of my deepest dreams, or if, like Mary the mother of Jesus, I will wait, storing up God's Word in my heart, and watch my dreams be crucified before they know resurrection.

I simply do not know. But then, being all-knowing is not my job.

Even at the height of Jesus' public recognition, he still possessed hidden hopes, dreams, and callings that no one around him could comprehend. He took some of those dreams with him all way to the cross.

What then do we do in hidden years with our unfulfilled dreams? Do we try to forget them? No, the holy place of hiddenness is where dreams and devotion thrive. Rather, we wait. The

God who is worthy of waiting upon is equally worthy of being entrusted with our dreams.

Keep the waters of your spirit sweet. Hidden years most often do not come with a clear expiration date. In their midst, most at some point wrestle against a sour substance called resentment. A close cousin of impatience, resentment is really mumbling in a tuxedo. And mumbling is really an accusation of negligence against God.

Unseen and uncelebrated, in the thick of anonymous seasons we must choose between one of two paths: we can become resentful and cynical, or we can become respectful and submitted. The first road leads to bitterness, the second to authority.

Though the preferred choice appears obvious, making that choice can be a sincere struggle. When our potential seems stifled, we can easily begin to believe that someone or something is standing in our way: our leaders are nearsighted or our parents are overprotective, that supervisor is just jealous or our spouse is holding us back, the old guard has lost vision or the new board lacks experience, the committee is obviously clueless or the system is seriously ingrown . . . the list could go on and on.

But is God's will really that fragile? Does he not foresee? Is he caught off guard? Is he unprepared? Though we are certainly affected by the decisions of others, in truth only one thing has the power to jeopardize our future: us. And few things can sabotage our God-given potential faster than a bitter spirit. Along with unmodified obedience, a sweet spirit is one of the most powerful guardians of tomorrow.

52 | finally, be still

Wait because he is worthy, keep your spirit sweet, and (finally) *befriend stillness.* To fully experience the incredible riches of hidden years, we must rediscover, reclaim, and probably redefine the word *rest.* That is R-E-S-T. For those unfamiliar with this odd, little collection of letters, we will first consult Webster for enlightenment:

> [1]**rest**\rest\ *noun* [Middle English, from Old English; akin to Old High German *rasta* rest and perhaps to Old High German *ruowa* calm] **1** : REPOSE, SLEEP; specifically : a bodily state characterized by minimal functional and metabolic activities. **2** : freedom from activity or labor. **3** : a place for resting or lodging. **4** : peace of mind or spirit.
>
> *intransitive verb* **1** : to get rest by lying down; *especially* : SLEEP. **2** : to cease from action or motion : refrain from labor or exertion. **3** : to be free from anxiety or disturbance.[1]

Most of us are severely rest-impaired and understandably so in a culture that touts busyness as one of its highest societal virtues. We rush to save time and hurry to stay on schedule. We go faster to get farther and speed up to get ahead.

Why do we value perpetual busyness? Where is it written that God values it too? Yet busyness is lauded in the community of faith as much as in the marketplaces of the world.

Spiritually this can be problematic. Besides how it obviously exhausts us emotionally and stresses us physically, busyness often poses as an imposter for self-discipline. When busy, we can easily mistake being productive for being disciplined when in reality we may just be driven—by deadlines, fear of failure, perfectionism, or the desire to avoid disapproval.

True, interior self-discipline exists even when the pressure is not on, when others' expectations are so low we could trip over them, when no one is looking, and when none are disappointed because (sadly) none are really interested. Such is the opportunity afforded us by anonymous seasons! There, enduring self-discipline has the opportunity to grow slowly, steadily, layer upon layer, forming within us a sure, trustworthy foundation that can bear the weight of power and influence with unflinching integrity. Since discipline is one of the key strengths God seeks to cultivate in us in hidden years, busyness can mask its absence in our lives, leaving us extremely vulnerable to temptations of appetite.

But perhaps the greatest danger of busyness is how it offers itself as a substitute in our lives for intimacy with others and especially with God. Intimacy is emotionally invasive; it requires knowing and being known. But the vulnerability and the self-denial that intimacy necessitates can often feel too costly. So we substitute *doing* for *knowing* and *giving* for *being known*. "We show our love in other ways," we reason. But intimacy has no other way. Without time, without attention, without listening, without touch, we can call it what we like, but it is not intimacy.

Have you ever wondered what God really wants from us? He just wants to be close. On a cross, his Son removed the barrier sin had placed between us, so now Father God stands with open arms, simply wanting to draw us near. And that is very hard to accomplish when we live life like a series of connected hundred-yard dashes.

All the strengths God cultivates in hidden years are not developed so that we can receive high marks one day on some heavenly report card. These strengths keep our hearts pure, our minds free, and our spirits focused so we can intimately commune with our Holy Father God and—seen or unseen—passionately pursue his will on earth.

So, slow down. Become still. Carve out and nurture a sacred space to rediscover rest.

Try taking long walks through the woods. Paint a picture no one else will see. Read the ancients by candlelight. Consider the stars at midnight. Wander through an art museum. Play the piano when only God can listen. Pick out a journal and take up a pen. Plant a garden and delight in dirt-covered hands.

Resist rushing and seize the opportunity in hidden years to discover how you were uniquely designed to walk intimately with God.

Have you ever felt hidden? If so, you are in Excellent Company.

The most influential life in all of history spent 90 percent of his days submerged in the unseen. During three mostly un-documented, undecorated decades, Father God empowered him to live an authoritative, obedient life and die an eternally fruitful death. How thankful we all can be that Jesus recognized the riches in uncelebrated seasons of his life.

Anonymous seasons are the surprising source of enduring spiritual strength. Savor the season! Respect its potential. When graced with hidden years, wait because he is worthy, keep the waters of your spirit sweet, be still . . . and *grow*.

epilogue
the last leaf

From my writing room on the second floor, I can almost touch the silver maple that towers gracefully over the eastern wall of our home. As I type these final words, only one faded, brown leaf remains on her weathered limbs. Bowing to winter's whispers, the tree has been releasing her rich foliage leaf by leaf for weeks.

Her submission to the season is her saving strength. Clinging tightly to abundance when the times call for emptiness would be self-sabotaging.

Through the window I watch as birds pick her branches clean. Cardinals, blue jays, sparrows, finches, and chickadees, with each staccato peck of their beaks, strip away whatever remains of summer's bountiful memory from the silver maple. Bare, her lean limbs can support the coming snow and ice. But that weight would be too much for her frame in all its fullness. Lighter is better for the deep work of winter.

So she bows. She bends. She surrenders to thinning and in doing so thickens her foundation for an even more glorious summer to come.

In the same way, submission to God's seasons will be our saving strength. To resist thinning is to risk collapse. The future is weighty, capable of crushing the unprepared.

When God's whispers call us to release being celebrated and embrace being hidden, wisdom would invite us to bow in submission and bend in anticipation. In surrendering our fullness, we will gain eternal strength.

The maple bows with ease, responding to nature's promptings like a skilled dance partner. Though we share the same Creator, bowing to him does not come as naturally to our willful hearts. We can resist and at times even resent following God's leadership into seasons of hiddenness. Instead, we prefer to preserve our visible fruitfulness forever, adding to it (but never subtracting from it) in increasing measure without resting, without waiting, without winter.

Perhaps that small word *our* captures one of the greatest misconceptions. Does the tree belong to itself? Does it produce fruit for its own consumption? No. The tree belongs to its Planter, and its fruit is meant to be shared.

The One who planted us—who gave us life and who sustains our very existence by his Word—will be faithful to grow us. Father knows best and would never sabotage his own. He is, after all, *good*. We are stewards, not owners, of the fruit he cultivates in our lives. Ultimately, that fruitfulness is to be given away in his Name, not hoarded and displayed for our own glory.

Jesus willingly was stripped of his divine glory and took the form of man. He then submitted to Father God's whispers guiding him into an extended anonymous season that concealed all signs of visible fruit from the waiting world for decades. But the harvest that grew from Jesus' submitted life can spiritually feed the whole world!

My soul longs to share in that harvest. Hidden in winter, growing in spring, fruitful in summer, or transitioning in the fall, may God do whatever is needed through whatever season he so chooses to somehow enable us to introduce others to the living hope found only in Jesus.

I leave you then with a short story that came to me years ago about a young boy obviously destined for greatness.

> Whenever I am disappointed with my spot in life, I stop and think about the little boy who was trying out for a part in a school play. His mother told me that he'd set his heart on being in it, though she feared he would not be chosen. On the day the parts were awarded, I went with her to collect him after school. The boy rushed up to her, eyes shining with pride and excitement. "Guess what, Mom," he shouted, and then said those words that will remain a lesson to me: "I've been chosen to clap and cheer."[1]

When we have been chosen to clap and cheer, may God find our spirits as sweet. Sweetness through hiddenness guarantees abundance in harvest in God's good and perfect time.

182

notes

Chapter 3. Quite Literally Formative
1. *Merriam-Webster's Collegiate Dictionary*, 10th ed., s.v. "hidden."

Chapter 9. It Is Time!
1. W. A. Elwell and P. W. Comfort, *Tyndale Bible Dictionary*, Tyndale Reference Library (Wheaton, IL: Tyndale, 2001).

Chapter 11. A Split Sky
1. C. S. Keener and InterVarsity Press, *The IVP Bible Background Commentary: New Testament* (Downers Grove, IL: InterVarsity, 1993).

Chapter 12. Affirmation from Above
1. See Revelation 4:5; 8:5; 11:19; 14:2; 16:18; and 19:6.

Chapter 15. The Desert?
1. Gerhard Kittel and Gerhard Friedrich, eds., *Theological Dictionary of the New Testament*, trans. Geoffrey W. Bromiley, 10 vols. (vol. 10 compiled by Ronald Pitkin) (Grand Rapids, MI: Eerdmans, 1964–1976; Logos Research Systems electronic edition), CD-ROM.

Chapter 16. To Be Tempted
1. James Swanson, *Dictionary of Biblical Languages with Semantic Domains: Greek (New Testament)*, (Oak Harbor, WA: Logos Research Systems, 1997), CD-ROM and e-book.

Chapter 17. Forty, One, and Three
1. The parallels between these fasts—as well as between Jesus' baptism and wilderness journey and the Israelites' deliverance through the Red Sea and desert wanderings—are rich and many, as the quantity of books on the subject confirms. These comparisons, however, are not the focus of our study. We are here examining Jesus' experience as an abounding source of insight in itself, not only so in comparison with other points in history.
2. Luke offers a different ordering of the second and third interaction, concluding his account with Jesus in Jerusalem. His emphasis seems to be geographical, while Matthew's appears chronological.

Chapter 19. The First Lure
1. Gerhard Kittel and Gerhard Friedrich, eds., *Theological Dictionary of the New Testament*, trans. Geoffrey W. Bromiley, 10 vols. (vol. 10 compiled by Ronald Pitkin) (Grand Rapids, MI: Eerdmans, 1964–1976; Logos Research Systems electronic edition), CD-ROM.
2. *Merriam-Webster's Collegiate Thesaurus*, 1988, 1996, s.v. "lure."

Chapter 25. The Preexisting Word
1. W. A. Elwell and P. W. Comfort, *Tyndale Bible Dictionary*, Tyndale Reference Library (Wheaton, IL: Tyndale, 2001).

Chapter 26. The Underrated Virtue
1. *Merriam-Webster's Collegiate Dictionary*, 10th ed. s.v. "self-control."
2. See 1 Timothy 3:2 and Titus 1:8; 2:2.
3. See Titus 2:5–6.

Chapter 30. The Second Lure
1. See Luke 2:21–32, 41.
2. See Luke 2:49; 19:41–44.
3. See Luke 2:36–38 and Matthew 26:62–67.
4. Matthew George Easton, *Easton's Bible Dictionary* (1897; Oak Harbor, WA: Logos Research Systems, 1996), CD-ROM.

Chapter 31. The Second Longing
1. Matthew Henry, *Matthew Henry's Commentary on the Whole Bible* (Peabody, MA: Hendrickson, 1991, 1994), CD-ROM.

Chapter 38. Reflections
1. Basilea Schlink, *I Found the Key to the Heart of God* (Minneapolis: Bethany, 1975), 47–48.

Chapter 39. The Third Lure
1. John 12:31; 14:30.
2. 2 Corinthians 4:4 KJV.
3. To reference another time such a multitude will be assembled, see Revelation 7:9.

Chapter 45. Submission-Based Authority
1. See John 9:28 and 8:39.
2. Luke 22:42.

Chapter 50. Only One
1. Genesis 3:6.

Chapter 51. Wait, and Keep Your Spirit Sweet
1. See 2 Samuel 5:4. See also R. Jamieson, A. R. Fausset, and D. Brown, *A Commentary, Critical and Explanatory, on the Old and New Testament* (Oak Harbor, WA: Logos Research Systems, 1997), CD-ROM.
2. See Genesis 12:1–4 and 21:1–5.
3. See Genesis 37:2, 5; 41:46–53; 45:4–6.
4. See Acts 7:20–34.
5. Esther became queen in 497 BC (see Esther 2:17–18), and she stood before the king begging him to stop the genocide of her race in 473 BC (see Esther 7:3–8:14). See R. B. Hughes and J. C. Laney, *Tyndale Concise Bible Commentary*, rev. ed. of *New Bible Companion* (Wheaton, IL: Tyndale, 2001).
6. Paul's conversion (see Acts 9) took place in AD 35. But he was not commissioned by the church at Antioch until sometime after AD 44 (see Acts 13:1–3).

Chapter 52. Finally, Be Still
1. *Merriam-Webster's Collegiate Dictionary*, 10th ed. s.v. "rest."

Epilogue: The Last Leaf
1. Forwarded to me via e-mail August 18, 2000. Original source is unknown.

"the insight of a theologian
and the imagination of a poet"

"the mind of a lawyer and
the voice of an angel"

"a dangerously gifted
communicator"

ALICIA BRITT CHOLE speaks nationally
and internationally to leaders, pastors,
professionals, college students, women,
and churches. All who have heard her
agree: Alicia is an unusually disarming
combination of realism and compassion,
intellect and vulnerability, humor and art.

Whether high-tech or antique, trendy or traditional, simple or
sophisticated . . . young and old alike describe Alicia's messages
as piercing but welcome surgeries. One pastor captured the
comments of many when he said, "My first thought was, *she
has such a gentle spirit.* My second thought was, *I think she just
removed my appendix!*"

Alicia would love to hear your reflections
on *anonymous: Jesus' hidden years and
yours.* To connect with Alicia, hear her
speak, learn more about her resources,
or order the 7-week DVD small group
reflective bible study for *Anonymous,*
visit www.truthportraits.com

CPSIA information can be obtained
at www.ICGtesting.com
Printed in the USA
LVOW08s0154090617
537463LV00003B/4/P